Making College

pay

How to Earn Money
While You're Still in School

Jon E. Carson

ADDISON-WESLEY PUBLISHING COMPANY
Reading, Massachusetts · Menlo Park, California
London · Amsterdam · Don Mills, Ontario · Sydney

Library of Congress Cataloging in Publication Data

Carson, Jon E.
  Making college pay.

  Includes index.
  1. Student-owned business enterprises—Management.
  2. New business enterprises—Management. I. Title.
  HD62.5.C37 1983   658.1'1'024375   83–11903
  ISBN 0–201–10820–8 (pbk.)

Set in 10-point ITC Zapf Light by Kingsport Press, Kingsport, TN
Cover design by Gary Fujiwara
Interior illustrations by Victoria Blaine

ISBN 0–201–10820–8
BCDEFGHIJ–DO–854

Second Printing, February 1984

This book is dedicated to my mother, who raised me alone against overwhelming odds and along the way rose from answering the mail to being editor-in-chief of *Gourmet* magazine despite never having received formal training or a college education. No one could ask for a better upbringing or a more inspiring parent. Her virtues of initiative, creativity, and courage are what this book is all about.

Character and initiative, properly balanced, are the basis of business success. Beginnings may be humble, but the results will be permanent if the spiritual grows with the material. One is the latch, the other the key; one is the flint, the other the steel.

—Roger Babson, 1960

ACKNOWLEDGMENTS

I started this book at the ripe old age of 21. Since I had never written a book before, I needed a lot of help from many people, and I want to thank them publicly for their assistance. Any omissions are purely accidental and are a result of my legendary forgetfulness.

First, in a general sense I would like to thank my present and past colleagues at both Yale and Babson for their patience with my time demands for this book and assorted ventures. A personal tribute to the Benzene Ring, who proved that a group can work in harmony despite what Clay says.

Special thanks to Richard Bishop, who was the first believer and never let me quit. A note of recognition to my partners in various businesses, Richard Taylor, David Tashjian, Jay Lustig, and Jim Tabner (sometimes referred to as "baloni"), for certainly without them it wouldn't have happened.

A gentleman whom I did business with, Paul Hirsch, is responsible for much of my personal growth, so much so that I even followed in his footsteps to Yale. Likewise my manager at Boeing, Bill Modestino, who deserves much of the credit for teaching me the finer art of "cutting a deal," not to mention a few tips on selling.

I am grateful to Steve Permut of the Yale School of Management for taking the time to review some of the material on marketing, and to a classmate, Barbara Brenner, for taking precious time to help me strengthen the chapter on accounting.

Typing was a horrendous problem for me (probably because I can't type), and a special thanks is due to Eileen Donahue, who knows these words backward and forward, since she typed a good portion of them. Also thanks to Mary Radford, who pushed me over the top with a timely interview at the NBC affiliate in Washington, D.C.

ACKNOWLEDGMENTS

There are three outstanding editors who in their spare time helped me immeasurably and whose enthusiasm was infectious. They are Alice Gochman, Bernice Levine, and Albert Levy. Thanks also to Marlene Mockel and Grace Lucas, who came through in the clutch on several occasions.

My cousin, Victoria Blaine, in Cambridge, Massachusetts, drew all the illustrations and was another clutch player who came through in the eleventh hour. I am blessed with a family of creative individuals.

Acknowledgments to John Zimmer ("Z"), who helped considerably in designing the chapter on accounting. Its contents bear his stamp.

A special acknowledgment to Ronny Jaques, who played a major role in my youth and who also took the picture on the back of the book.

Thanks to Mrs. Lillian Christenson, who financed me into the sneezing powder business in fifth grade and thus sparked my initial venture into student enterprise.

A mention of appreciation to Joan Ryan at Yale, who kept me going through a tough first semester at graduate school.

Last and absolutely not least, a special thanks to my editor at Addison-Wesley, Ellie Neville, who believed in the idea as much as I did and whose enthusiasm has been contagious. This book is in large part due to her efforts.

Thanks to all of you.

Let's do it again sometime.

J. C.

CONTENTS

PREFACE

This book addresses some fundamental problems in our educational system—specifically, a tuition cost squeeze and the dilemma of liberal arts students who cannot get jobs with the skills that have been honed in college. Though starting and running your own student business is by definition entrepreneurial, this book does not attempt to teach entrepreneurship, because it cannot be taught. Entrepreneurship is an inherent feeling of individuality and initiative. However, student business owners need not be true entrepreneurs. The true entrepreneur takes much greater risks. Students can if they wish, but in the college world the risk of starting a student business is generally much lower than that of a full-fledged venture that you might start later in life. Most student businesses are service oriented, not capital intensive, and the risk is usually calculated in time rather than dollars. Even with a failed business that you spent three weeks of your time getting launched, you at least have some valuable experience that your backgammon-playing counterpart across the dormitory hallway does not. Ultimately, that experience will pay dividends when you graduate and look for a job. So you see, in student business there really are no losers.

Most of us who graduate from college will end up in the private sector. Those who go to the non-profit or public sector will see that these areas are becoming increasingly like their private sector counterpart, with objectives, strategies, budgets, and goals. Consequently, this book is also meant to give a simplistic overview of all the tools used in business, from formulating strategy to financial controls. These are skills that you will inevitably be called upon to use in both your private life and your professional career. As I mentioned, this book doesn't attempt to teach entrepreneurship, but it gives you the tools and advice with which you can run your own business. For those of you who have dreams of eventually running your own enterprise as a career, running a student business gives you an excellent opportunity to discover the pros and cons at an early age. After all, one never really knows until trying, and if it's not meant for you, better to know now rather than in ten years when there is more at risk.

Student businesses come in all different shapes, sizes, and approaches. There is really no definitive right or wrong way to run a business, but there are guidelines that are best adhered to. It is important to have a strategy consistent with your objectives, and cash controls to ensure that you get the money you've earned. I have broken the fundamentals down into segments that are discussed individually. At the end I've pulled them all together to show how a business owner integrates these functions into a smooth-running, tightly controlled, strategically planned business that generates profits and provides part-time employment for other students.

Finally, from my own experience, I can say that there are few thrills to match my feeling of accomplishment as I took an idea and watched it grow into a successful money-making operation. The feeling of confidence and that "I've done it!" is one I never was able to match by getting an A in a course. Unlike a college course where a half-dozen students are likely to get a B or better, there are probably few people on your campus who run their own business. You will be distinctive. Think about it: if you ran into two college students, one who said he had gotten an A in biology and the other who said he was running a $20,000 business on three campuses with four employees, whom would you be more interested in meeting? I think you'd find that the student business magnate would strike your curiosity much more than the biology student.

I hope you find the following pages as stimulating to read as they were to write. But the ultimate test is whether you go out and actually give it a whirl. After all, you'll never know how successful you might be unless you try.

CHAPTER 1

Starting a
Student Business

There exists in this country an emerging crisis of education that holds the potential to be the beginning of an educational revolution. This book is presented as a possible answer to that crisis, so that you may overcome the two hurdles that have recently arisen in our educational system.

The first hurdle is a financial one. College costs are going up across the country, ranging from 6 percent (in rare cases) to 15 percent (in many cases). But tuition increases are not so unusual—after all, 6- to 15-percent tuition hikes have been going on for years, as my poor mother can well testify. The difference now is that instead of being 10-percent increases on $3,000 tuition and fees ($300) they are 12-percent increases on $10,000 tuition and fees ($1,200). Estimates now place the cost of a four-year college education for a child going to a private school away from home at $40,000 after taxes. That translates to $60,000 to $90,000 of income after federal and state income taxes—a lot of bread.

But the story isn't over yet. In times of budgetary restraint (which I'm all for) the funding for guaranteed student loans and federal assistance is being cut (which I'm not for). The fact of the matter is that funding is going down in real dollars and costs are going up. Who's in the middle? You and your family. The consequent fact is that the equality of opportunity and education upon which Jefferson and our forefathers built this country is in jeopardy, and our generation will be the first to suffer.

Let us direct our attention to another crisis in American collegiate education. The liberal arts programs at most schools today are not providing graduates with the skills employers are looking for. Let's face it, a degree in art history is intellectually stimulating, but that discipline doesn't always help when it comes to getting a job after graduation. This is compounded by the fact that your first job is always the hardest to get because you have little or no track record. Although you may be heavily involved in campus activities, you'd be surprised how they all look the same in a stack of 200 résumés on a desk in a personnel department. The cold truth is that if you want a good, above-average job out of college you have to find a way to stand out from the crowd. This particularly holds true in large universities with graduating classes of 3,000 or more. You can bet that when IBM comes on campus to recruit, the interview line is going to be long and competitive.

Severe financial strain and a way of standing out in a crowd are the two big problems for college students today. However, there is a terrific solution that has worked for thousands of college students—starting and/or running a student business—and that's what this book is all about. A student business is the epitome of what this country stands for: innovation and initiative. Entrepreneurship and innovation are what have made this country great, and if it worked for others it can work for you.

Take me, for example. I went to Babson College as the proverbial Mr. Average. I wasn't a particularly good student. The soccer coach gave me about 10 minutes during tryouts before telling me to hit the showers, so I wasn't a great athlete. All in all I was just another nice kid, of which there were 1,300 others at Babson. When I graduated with a C average (and I might add that there was some discussion as to whether I would even graduate), I got one of the most competitive jobs in the market. I went to work for the Computer Services and Consulting Division of the Boeing Company, a job for which there were over 200 applicants. Since then I applied to graduate business schools and was admitted to several schools, including Yale, where I am now studying.

How did I do it? I became heavily involved in student businesses. It wasn't particularly hard; after all, it isn't like running a multinational corporation, where you have to concern yourself with interest and currency rates, labor unions, and such high-level problems. In college there is less direct competition, so running a student business is comparatively easy.

Because there is relatively little competition, the opportunity to distinguish yourself is considerably larger. When most people are asked to describe those who distinguished themselves in college, they think of high grades. If most of the student body thinks that way, then you have several thousand students who want to stand out with high grades and only a limited number of high grades to get. Professors rarely give the whole class an A. Therefore, the answer is to find another way to stand out that is equally impressive and probably easier. An added bonus would be to find something that would make money for you while you're having fun. After all, students usually don't get $1,000 in cash for doing well in school. You can see what I'm leading up to. A student business makes money for you and shows future employers the kind of stuff you're made of.

If you were seeking a motivated person to join your company as the new junior associate, wouldn't you be impressed by someone who walked into your office and said: "Hello, Mr. Carson. I started a business in my spare time in college and grossed $40,000 in three years, employing three people part-time. I was wondering whether you might consider me for the job that I saw you advertise." You bet you would!

Look at it this way. How many people in your class at school are going to get excellent grades this year? Ten, twenty, maybe fifty, if you go to a large school. Now how many are going to take the trouble to start their own business? Probably not very many. What's more, how many students are going to make money while studying? Again, not very many. Besides, you will learn a lot more about business fundamentals by owning a business than you will in most of your basic business or economics courses. So, now you can see why you will be unique in the eyes of any prospective employer.

Let me give you another example. A friend of my mom's had a son, Bob, who attended an Ivy League college in the Northeast. Bob had an idea involving birthday cakes. Many of his classmates were from out of state, and for the first time were celebrating their birthdays without Mom and Dad. They didn't care so much, but you can bet Mom and Dad did. Bob managed to get a mailing list of everybody's parents. Cleverly, he put together a form letter that was addressed to Mumsie. It told her that if she wanted to have Junior remember the folks back home on birthday day, Bob would deliver a cake to Junior's door, candles, song, and all, for just $9.95. Now what kind of Mom is going to turn down a deal like that? To make a long story short, not many did, and young Bob grossed several thousand dollars that year, taking home a healthy profit. When Bob went to look for a job, he got

4

several offers from Fortune 500 companies and eventually settled on a large Wall Street brokerage firm. The point is this: Bob's experience showed that he had initiative, maturity, and a head on his shoulders, which are three of the most marketable points you can offer to any employer.

On the other hand, if Bob decides to go the entrepreneur route full time after he gets out of school, he will have several lessons under his belt at a relatively low cost. After all, would you rather make a $100 mistake now or a $10,000 one when you go big time? When you own a student business, your mistakes are relatively small in terms of dollars, but the lessons learned stay with you for the rest of your life. The lesson learned from a mistake frequently is worth the price you pay. It is important when you have made a boo-boo to step back and say, "How is this applicable to business as a whole?" "What lesson can I learn from this experience?"

It happened to me. In my junior year of college I had a flourishing publishing business. My partner and I decided to diversify and expand into a small gum vending machine operation in upstate New York, where his family lived. Now this was 200 miles from Boston, where we were attending college. Although the day-to-day operations were done by friends, we never seemed to be getting anywhere, and we had invested some hard-earned money from another venture in this project. The operation was barely profitable, and we never saw it. The lessons we learned: (1) Never expand your business so far that you lose control of how it performs, and (2) never diversify into fields where you have no experience, unless you feel that you have an unusual edge over the competition. I can assure you that these are two lessons I shall never forget.

This book shows you some of the basic areas of business with which you must be familiar in order to compete successfully. The alternative is to find out the hard way. Since I've pulled some real boners in my business career, I can tell you that reading a book like this is the easier of the alternatives. This book assumes that most of you have little or no practical business experience; it serves as an introduction to the fundamentals to give you a feel for some of the tools you need to get a profitable business going, which doubtless most of you will do. If you feel you are sufficiently strong in some of the areas that will be discussed later on, bear with me or skip ahead to the next section. However, because most people don't have the business background, included are even the most basic concepts of marketing, advertising, finance, sales, accounting, and a few others. Amazingly, you might even learn to like this stuff. Who knows, it might even make you rich someday.

To start with, I think it is important to define what a business is, so you are not confused about what your role will be.

Seem funny?

I had a friend who was approached by owners of a local pizza shop who wanted to have him represent them at the local college. "It will be just *like* having your own business on campus," they told him. My friend, Jay, went merrily along with the idea, and all was fine until he suggested a more costly way to deliver the pizzas, which would keep them hotter. His employers wouldn't go along with him on the premise that he worked on commission and the decisions were up to the owner. Jay had misjudged his role in the operation. He wasn't the boss and didn't make the decisions, so it really *wasn't* "like having his own business." He was paid a commission; thus, he was considered a labor cost to the pizza shop owners. Jay started his own pizza delivery business, making the pizzas the cost, rather than his own labor services. He actually did quite well, because in using his more expensive delivery system, he virtually wrapped up the entire pizza market on campus (taking a sizable share from his former employer). After he had established himself on his first campus venture, he knew the daily operations and where they could be improved to enhance profitability. Once he had the expertise, he began adding nearby colleges to his delivery runs. When he had reached a point where he did not have the time to personally supervise the operations at each campus, he hired a manager for each college. By instituting various controls, he assured himself that the managers could not break away from him and start their own pizza businesses. He gave each manager a percentage of the revenues to pay their own salaries and to pay commissions to the delivery boys. Jay ended up supervising the overall operations, letting the managers deal with the day-to-day routines and headaches. He eventually expanded to nine surrounding colleges and grossed about $70,000 a school year in sales while he was a junior in college.

See? It isn't too hard.

A business, student-run or otherwise, is an operation engaged in selling a service or product. (Or it can be in a miscellaneous category that involves both.) For purposes of argument, rental businesses will be considered a product service. There are inflows and outflows of cash. Of the outflows, there are two types. The first is a direct cost, which is the cost of the product or service that you are offering. The second is overhead, which is the cost of doing business—for example, your salary, telephone expenses, office rent, and gasoline. The difference between the inflows and the outflows should be a profit. Sometimes, frankly, it is a loss, but approaching this with a negative attitude is counterproductive, so let's not dwell on it.

When starting a business, either as a summer job or on campus during school, it is the direct cost that you must drive down in order to be competitive. This will lead to a low selling price, since your overhead is usually minimal compared to that of your "big-time" competition. After all, why should anyone buy from you if a reputable merchant has the same product for the same price? It is your reduced price that will initially draw people to you. The reason you can sell at a reduced price is that you are buying whatever you are selling at less than retail price.

How can you sell at less than retail price? The answer is pure and simple—bulk. When you buy by the case or carton, you receive what is known as a quantity discount. This is done to entice you to buy more. The more you buy, the better the price gets, until you reach a limit where you've got the price down as far as the dealer is willing to go. Of course, you have a risk/return tradeoff in that once you buy your product you are stuck with it, and you had better be sure you're going to sell the damn things or you will face what is called an "inventory write-off." Two little tips on smart shopping: (1) It might behoove you to find out which dealer the local merchant is buying from, because ideally you would like to get a wholesale price. (2) It never hurts to tell the people you deal with that you represent a large market and will be a very profitable customer over the long run. Wholesalers aren't stupid. They realize that you will serve the local market much better than the local merchant who is busy selling a dozen other products anyway. The lower that direct cost is, the better off you are. The difference between what you pay for your product and the going rate is the margin with which you have to work to cover overhead and profit.

Dan Conan, from the University of Texas, is a good example of what I'm talking about. Dan got an idea from an old high school buddy in Portland, Maine. The idea was to sell hot pretzels at sporting events. Dan went around to local stores and got a variety of prices for large bags of pretzels. The prices ranged from 18 cents to 26 cents per pretzel, and Dan planned on selling them for 75 cents. However, Dan wasn't satisfied with his cost of goods (pretzels), and he continued to look for a better supplier. Finally his persistence paid off, and he found a baker who not only sold Dan the pretzels for 15 cents but also gave him a warmer display box so that they would be heated. Dan took home about $900 per year on sales of approximately $1,400, which isn't millions, but it did provide him pocket money with enough left over to pay his bookstore bill.

Obviously, the lower you keep your overhead the more money you are going to make, and the higher the overall quality of your lifestyle is going to be. This is the secret to a part-time business.

Low direct costs + Low overhead = Lots of profits

See? It's a lot easier than you thought it was.

Here is another example: Nineteen-year-old Jason "Snapper"

Montant started a company that bought kegs of beer in bulk, 20 to 30 at a time. He sold them to fraternities and dorms at colleges in the area. Jason hired a senior who had a Jeep, rented a U-Haul, and offered delivered-to-your-door service. (It is important to check local liquor regulations to see if delivering liquor is legal before trying this one.)

Anyone who has ever had the misfortune of trying to get a keg of beer (which weighs about 120 pounds) knows what a royal nuisance these things are. Not only are kegs heavy, but few breweries bother to put handles on them, so they are awkward as well. Jason added a $2 surcharge, which everyone was only too happy to pay because he had a unique service. Consequently, Jason was making it on both ends—the spread between his cost and the market price as well as his surcharge. Again, as in the example of the pizza business, Jason took a good idea and perfected it on his home campus. Once he had the operation perfected, he expanded onto nearby campuses. Usually a business that works well on one campus stands a good chance of being successful on others. By expanding, Jason increased his volume to such an extent that he dropped his keg costs by over 20 percent. This went directly into his profits, since there was no need to drop his price—he was already competitive with local merchants.

(The only exception to the rule of not charging more than the current market price is when you offer a product or service that is not currently available in the local marketplace. Discretion is the vital element here because you don't want to price yourself out of the market and start getting a reputation for being greedy. On the other side of the coin, don't sell yourself short. A good example here would be Jason, who, because he offered a unique service, namely *delivering* kegs, had a unique product-service.)

Jason told me after he sold his business that his one regret was not realizing what a captive market he had. "If only I had charged $2 or $3 more per barrel," he lamented to me one day when we were discussing the problems of the world over a beer. It took Jason a lot of hours to get this one off the ground, but in the end he grossed just over $20,000.

The Three Types of Student Businesses

Essentially there are three types or categories of so-called student businesses: service, product-service, and those that escape any one classification, which I shall call miscellaneous. Following are some very basic definitions and examples of each.

Service Business

This type of enterprise involves selling a service, for example, furniture moving, painting, or landscaping. Because the services involve labor as a principal cost, they are considered labor-intensive. Sometimes you will have to buy equipment such as paint brushes or even a lawn mower (which these days is no longer a drop in the bucket), but nonetheless these costs comprise a relatively small part of your overall expenses and are usually one-time costs (you don't go out and buy a new lawn mower every time you mow another lawn). Consequently, starting a business of this nature generally involves a small investment.

Bill Litefield started a very profitable house-painting business with about $50 in materials in Fairfield County, Connecticut. By the second summer he had expanded to running four crews and was rumored to be pocketing about $10,000 a summer. Bill ran a very tight ship and was uncannily accurate in projecting his costs when he gave quotes. Essentially, Bill had minimal overhead, which his quotes reflected. His prices were always 15 to 20 percent lower than the professional painting services, which not only had higher overhead costs because of phone, rental, and secretarial services, but also had higher labor costs because they hired men who painted for a living. Bill, who had college and high-school kids working for him, usually paid 10 to 15 percent over minimum wage, while the professional services paid $10 to $15 an hour. Thus, Bill competed with similar services at a reduced cost. But he was smart enough to realize that he had to do work that was as good as, if not better than, the competition. His first summer he ran his operation with one crew, promoting his name and getting a good list of references from people who were satisfied with his work. By the second summer, the groundwork had been laid, and he had established a reputation for quality. Then he almost always won his bids on price, and because of the increase in business he expanded to four crews. This is a good example of a simple, profitable service business.

If Bill and others can do it, so can you!

Product-Service

Product-service-oriented businesses are just extensions of the service business with the added feature of providing a product. A pizza or beer delivery business, a refrigerator rental business, or even Bob's birthday cake business would all be good examples of a product-service business. Basically, these businesses offer things you can get anywhere, but essentially the reason people buy is for the service; the fact that someone will come right to their door is the reason they buy the pizza from that person. It isn't any better and usually costs more than the local pizza shop, but people like the convenience.

One of the reasons this type of business is especially successful on college campuses is that most students do not enjoy the benefits of a car. If you are one of the lucky few who have a car, you can take many of the products offered in town and simply bring them on campus. It's not easy for the students to go to the store, so you bring the store to the students. (This might be a good way to convince Dad that the family's extra car might contribute to your educational process at college.)

Probably the most lucrative business I ever had (relative to the amount of time it took) was a refrigerator rental service that I started at the end of my freshman year. If beauty is simplicity, then this one was the *Mona Lisa* of student enterprise. A classmate and I canvassed the local colleges to sign up prospective renters. After we had a rough idea of how many units we needed, we added a margin for stragglers (some people are notorious for saying no, but when they see their neighbors getting their own refrigerators, they change their minds. When we had a final figure, we went to a wholesaler who rented out the refrigerators in bulk and who drop-shipped them on campus. All in all, we spent about four hours a day for five days, and presto! The work was done. The rest was a two-day wholesale pickup effort in May. A side benefit was that we got a deposit from all our customers that was used to finance some of my other projects. It didn't occur to me until a few years later that this might be illegal. However, it seemed just plain stupid to go out and borrow money with all that deposit money sitting in the bank. In all, we had worked about 25 to 30 hours for some very good money. It didn't make millionaires out of us but, then again, we had the rest of the school year to do that.

Miscellaneous

This term is vague, I know, but there is a group of ideas that by the very nature of their existence deserve mentioning. The point of discussing this group is to open your mind to inspirations that fall outside the two previously mentioned groups. Rather than describe this group, which is virtually impossible to define, here are a few examples of unusual ideas.

Steve and Gary are two classmates who started a business in the real estate field, which is neither a service nor a product as one thinks of pizzas or refrigerators. With money they borrowed from classmates and family, they made a down payment on a house in Newport, Rhode Island, made several home improvements, and sold it at a capital gain, which is taxed at a considerably lower rate than ordinary profits. (We will cover taxes in a later chapter.) An unusual enterprise, to say the least. Needless to say, Steve and Gary now know as much about real estate as anyone else. Steve, incidentally, was offered and accepted a position with Cushman and Wake-field, a prestigious commerical real estate firm. As a result, Steve made two or three times what most of the rest of us earn. Today he is at the Columbia Business School getting his M.B.A.

One of the most interesting projects I ever had was in the publishing field. In my particular case the revenues were from selling advertisements, which are neither a service nor a product; rather they are an intangible. My business primarily published soccer game programs for New England colleges and universities, as well as the NCAA national soccer championship program for Division III. We made our money by selling advertisements, which is one way to start off in the publishing business. What we did was to establish a niche in the advertising market—we were the only media vehicle for anyone who wanted to reach the youth soccer market. Additionally, we were able to pick up advertising from three local merchants who wished to show support of particular schools or colleges. Also, we could boast that we were "new" and "exciting"— positive attributes in the advertising world. Certainly, there was no selling of a product (the actual programs themselves were given away), and it would be stretching things to refer to advertising as a service in the conventional sense.

After all this, you are still probably thinking, "These are great ideas in unique situations, but how in the world am I going to start a venture like these?"

There is at least one very good reason you should be able to start a successful business, and it goes back to some of the points mentioned earlier.

Primary among these is overhead. Remember that the merchant in town has overhead that he cannot avoid. The rent has to be paid, the sales clerk has to be compensated, and the telephone company doesn't give away its services either. All of these things are easily avoidable if you run your show out of your dorm or apartment. The exception might be a phone, but you would have that anyway for personal use, so there is no additional expense. Automatically there is a competitive advantage over the person in town because you have a comparable or better margin if you both buy from the same wholesaler.

That brings up the second point: the margin between your selling price and cost of goods. In fact, if you shop around you might find a better wholesaler with a better price than your big-time competition has been able to get.

A third advantage in addition to having more control over your costs, is that you are closer to your market. You live on campus or in town and see neighbors on a personal basis, so you can pay more attention to their needs. The personal touch, one of the most important elements of starting a business, is a strategy that I will discuss later in this book.

So, essentially, the trick to getting your business out of the starting blocks is to get your merchandise or labor services cheaper than the prices at which the merchant in town can get them. In the case of service businesses, basic labor is pretty constant (minimum wage is minimum wage for everyone), so you have to count on your reduced overhead to give you a competitive pricing advantage. The smaller the margin between cost and selling price, the more widgets (or whatever) you must sell. This is what economics professors mean when they talk about high-volume/low-margin industries. This may sound like the most obvious statement in the world, but you would be amazed how many people try to start low-margin/average-volume businesses and can't understand why the moola isn't rolling in when everything looked so good on paper. It's important to remember that the lower you "jam" down your costs, the wider that margin gets. Once you have a decent margin to work with, the next step is sales. The trick is not to get so greedy that you start selling an inferior product that your buyers lose faith in. The implications of this tactic are obvious: short-term profits and long-term bankruptcy after your customers decide to go elsewhere.

A great example of this is a certain fraternity (which shall go nameless) that put out a desk blotter every year. This is a cardboard desk covering that has advertising on the top of it and that is distributed around dorms in colleges. The sales pitch is that most students spend a great deal of their time at their desks (I was never among that majority), and what better place to put an advertisement? Well, this frat used to make an estimated $500 to $800 each year on the blotter, free cash, practically no work. Just sign up the same old advertisers, collect the money, and send the copy to the printer. Then they stopped distributing the blotters around dorms where they didn't have any members residing. Because these guys all lived in one or two dorms, the distribution was incomplete to say the least. They eventually lost some advertisers and got a pretty shoddy reputation among those in the business of buying and selling advertising as a result. The importance of this example is always to think long-term or take the chance of getting a reputation for being a fly-by-nighter.

An example of what happens when you do think long-term involves Alpha Kappa Psi, a Babson fraternity. This frat had several enterprising lads who decided it was high time the college had a directory listing all the names and phone numbers of the students. In the second year of the publication, the president of the fraternity decided to take a calculated risk. It was decided to spend an additional $200 on layout to improve the aesthetics of the directory, as well as to spend an extra $300 to switch to glossy paper. The end result was that advertising sales the next year improved dramatically as advertisers saw what a slick publication the directory was, and these guys easily made back their investment even though they had forfeited profits the year before to do so. It takes maturity to forfeit today's quick profits for tomorrow's higher or long-term earnings. Starting a student business sometimes involves deferred gratification and in the process you learn about the risks and returns of making an investment in yourself. Needless to say, this is another selling point to potential employers when you interview. It is a great way to get some upper management experience before you go to work for someone else full-time.

By now you have a rough idea of what small enterprise is about and why the odds are in your favor because of your low overhead. The examples given so far (all of which are true) are meant to show the range that part-time businesses can cover, although some of them, by virtue of their growth, could gradually evolve into more than just part-time projects. Some of these businesses were formed under unique situations and may prove to be impossible to do in your particular school or town. That's all right; there are a million and one other ideas out there. Some are in the remainder of this book, but most aren't. Basically, the main reason so many examples are included is to show that it is quite possible to start your own business and make some terrific money as well as get hands-on experience.

There is one last thing that you should always keep in mind. The complexity or absolute size of your venture really does not matter. What matters is that you *learn!* That's not to say that you should deliberately slow the growth of your business, but if you have an interesting idea that has limited potential, go ahead and give it a shot. A buddy of mine, Scott Banholtzer, started a business in squash racquets and accessories, which really had limited potential, but he went ahead anyway, enjoyed it a lot, and learned a lot about cash management. Now he's a senior associate at a large insurance firm in Wisconsin. Let's face it, 99 percent of you don't have the resources or the experience to make millions at your age. So why not start a simple lawn service, or a painting service like Will did, and learn from it, make it grow, and try out different ideas and strategies? The more you learn from it, the greater edge you will have over your peers later on when it really counts, whether it be as president of your own company or as vice-president of strategic planning for RCA. That is one of the most important points of this book.

CHAPTER 2

Getting an Idea

The *idea* is the first of a three-part process that takes place when a business is started. Getting the idea includes refining it into a workable concept. The second stage is *implementation* (which is discussed in detail in Chapter 3) into reality, generally the most difficult of the three parts. The third part is the day-to-day *running of the business* once it is off the ground. Without the idea, however, steps two and three can never take place.

An idea, new or old, is the seed of any new business. The title of this chapter may seem slightly deceptive, because it implies that I'm actually going to show you how to get an idea. In fact, that is about as realistic as telling you that I can teach you how to be intelligent. Obviously, I can't tell you *how* to dream up wild schemes like selling Indian wampum beads to radical 1960s types employing a push-pull marketing strategy, using coupons inserted into E Z Wider smoking papers sold at the counters of local health food shops. However, what *is* possible is to show how you can get yourself in a better frame of mind that will stimulate not only the quantity but the quality of crazy ideas that come your way.

If you are one of those people who just don't have much of a gift for creativity and imagination, you will have to revert to the highest form of flattery: imitation. Imitating a successful idea doesn't make you any less successful than if the idea is an original. The main impetus behind starting a campus business is to learn, which you will do in either case. And it isn't the initial idea so much as it is the ability to carry it out that makes a successful business. After all, who cares how many great ideas you get if you never try one out or don't do much with the ones you do attempt? If I had a nickel for every idea one of my friends has had and promptly forgot about with the thought, "Aw, that will never work," or "I'll try it some other time," I'd be a very rich man. There are a lot of people who have great ideas but never bother to try to implement them. What a waste of creative talent! If only these people knew how many of us are lucky if we come up with one good idea every couple of years, they might appreciate what a gift they have. Because the idea is the original

seed of any new venture, it can be either watered and culti-
vated till it bears fruit or allowed to die.

The end of the chapter discusses some of the ideas I've
had, but because my hands were full with other ventures, I
never got a chance to try them out. You might want to try
some out or just get a feel for some of the opportunities that
are out there in the campus marketplace.

Getting It Going

One method that has worked for me has a built-in filtering
process to weed out the slightly left-of-crazy brainstorms. Try
this. The minute you get an idea that makes any kind of sense,
write it down. Then put it in the back of your mind. Whenever
you're doing something that doesn't require much mental
effort (such as riding a bus or attending your basket-weaving
class), think about your idea and try to motivate yourself to
see the best possible results the idea could get if everything
went well. This gets the adrenaline going and keeps you from
letting your idea die a slow death of neglect.

After getting the general concept straight in your mind,
you should try it out on a few friends or professors. It never
hurts to get a second, third, or tenth opinion of an idea. It
is a lot easier than you may think to overlook something that
may be very obvious to someone else—such as the reality
that you *do* need the administration's permission before starting a Sunday morning Bloody Mary delivery service on campus. My mother is a firm believer in the old adage that so
very often the obvious is overlooked. If you learn to recognize
this, you will improve the odds of success of your venture
considerably.

After you have bounced your scheme off a few people, with
some positive reinforcement and helpful suggestions, you are
ready to start laying the groundwork. Often, along the way,
a few people might express interest in going in with you as
a partner, which is a nice benefit. One idea that I had was
to take a bartending course that Harvard Student Agencies

(a Harvard student business organization) offered in Cambridge and market it in the suburbs where it was not offered. While discussing the possible pros and cons with my roommate, Harry Scoble, I realized that he was as enthusiastic as I was, and presto! The incredible team of Scoble and Carson was born. The business was a complete flop. Actually, the fault was neither Harry's nor mine. Rather, Harvard Student Agencies unexpectedly canceled the marketing program we had devised after we had test-marketed it at Wellesley College. We lost considerable amounts of time and our fixed costs. The lesson there was never to risk more than you can afford to lose.

Need Perception

So far I've told you a little bit about what to do when you feel a brainstorm nibbling away inside you, but that doesn't help you get on track to get the idea itself. To get into a more productive frame of mind, think "need perception." This is an academic marketing term for the process of just figuring out what people want and then giving it to them. Honestly, it's that easy. If you think about what things you might want and are willing to pay for, all sorts of great ideas can come your way.

A good example would be Jason, who had the keg delivery business. Jason just got plain fed up with having to get kegs himself. Finally, after failing to find anyone who would deliver kegs right to his door, Jason decided it was high time that someone did, and the rest is history.

Another friend of mine, Ken Wadsworth, did this in an imaginative fashion. In advertising to the campus market, local advertisers had a limited number of vehicles to carry their advertising, such as the campus newspaper or my soccer programs. Ken decided to offer a whole new service: non-print media for advertising. Kenny decided to set up a slide projector in the main dining hall that switched slides every four seconds. The advertising slides were sandwiched between slides of assorted candid shots of life around campus to maintain viewers' interest. He offered regional merchants as well as the local campus entrepreneurs 15 exposures per meal at so many dollars per set of ten meals. By perceiving what his clients needed, Ken came up with a great idea using plenty of imagination. (Now this particular venture employed plenty of thought and imagination and many of us couldn't come up with anything so unique to a limited advertising media problem; but that doesn't mean you can't try!) The idea has since been picked up with success at Georgetown University, in Washington, D.C.

Every so often you probably find yourself thinking, "Wow, I wish someone would sell this because I would buy it." At times like these you should realize that if no one else is doing it, why not you? Most important is the second part: "Why not you?" The vast majority of people just forget about the idea and let what could become the beginning of a great adventure die.

Obviously your idea must appeal to a large enough market. If you think you're one of many who might want some particular product or service, then away you go. But just because *you* have a need doesn't mean the world shares it with you. If you can't find anyone who will rent you a South American bird cage, kiki bird and all, don't think you've found one of the last sure bets to make a million. A little more market research may be in order. You may find that you have an isolated need that most of your peers don't share with you. But if you find that your dorm might go for something like a soda machine, owned by you, in the basement, you might have something.

Brainstorming

Brainstorming is a technique that many professional problem solvers use to get ideas. Brainstorming can involve as few as two people, but generally it is more effective with several. Too many people and things get hectic, but with four or five people, you might still get the quantity of suggestions that a large group brings with less of the confusion. Basically, a brainstorming session involves a group of people sitting around throwing out ideas, most of which are so weird that they defy imagination. However, by sheer force of numbers, a few good imaginative ideas come out. Sometimes you can even take a totally off-the-wall suggestion and apply it to another concept. Following the law of averages, if you throw out 100 ideas, two or three good ones are bound to be workable. Let me give you an example.

A professional problem-solving group was discussing the problem of energy-efficient houses. One of the members of the group remarked that much heat could be saved if only the roof could change color like a weasel that is white in the summer and brown in the winter. As you know, white reflects sunlight and dark colors absorb it. Obviously there is a flaw in this suggestion. Roofs simply do not change color. A second member of the group commented that a flounder does a similar transformation. When in the vicinity of white sand it appears white, but around dark sand it appears distinctly darker. The reason, he continued, was that there are little white dots on the flounder that expand when it is near white sand and contract when it is near dark sand. When the flounder is dark, there are still hundreds of little white dots; it's just that you can't see them because they have contracted so much. The group eventually developed a roof that contained miniature white plastic balls under a black covering. When the roof gets hot, the little white balls expand and come to the top to reflect the sunlight. When it gets cold, the balls contract and submerge under the black roofing.

This example shows how a crazy idea can finally evolve into something that makes sense.

The technical name for this brainstorming method is *synectics*. The foregoing example was borrowed from *Synectics,* by William Gordon (New York: Collier-Macmillan, 1961), which deals primarily with problem solving. It is better not to use this method in the actual conception of a business, since if results don't come speedily, everyone might go home frustrated with no motivation to come back. Once you've agreed on the idea, synectics can be used to solve a particular problem of operations where, as partners with a commitment, you all share a common bond to keep yourselves coming back to the second and third sessions.

Synectics is probably the most technical method of churning out ideas. In brainstorming, the secret is never to reject anyone's idea; it may ultimately lead in a more fruitful direction. If you attempt a brainstorming session, always try to modify the absurd and keep the strength of any central concept. Don't overdo it, though. You might be labeled as some sort of creative weirdo if you've been having two brainstorming sessions a day for six months just because it worked the first time.

Sometimes you can get the beginnings of an idea and just let it sit in the back of your mind. You may have a great idea with a small problem that prevents its development. Sometimes if you sit on a problem and mull it over, the answer eventually surfaces in much the same way that, when you least expect it, you remember someone's name that you couldn't remember a week ago. Suddenly for no apparent reason it comes to mind, usually at the most obscure time. Keep it on your mind, but don't force yourself to concentrate on it. Try to let your subconscious work out the problems. If this doesn't work after a week or two, as a final resort to find a solution, have a brainstorming session.

The Need for New Ideas

Although imitation is the highest form of flattery, you should be wary of copying anyone who might later *compete* against you for two reasons. First, you are inviting trouble because someone who is already in business will usually have more experience than you. This is not to be underestimated, because there is no lesson as important as hands-on experience. Second, student-run businesses can't operate well against head-to-head competition because the profit margins aren't big enough to sustain cutthroat prices, which is usually what takes place in small markets such as these. Big markets can handle competition because there is enough pie to go around, but small markets don't have enough goodies to feed more than one or possibly two enterprises. There are some exceptions, such as painting services, which compete in a generally large market within several towns or counties. Painting businesses are good examples of businesses that do operate (and successfully) within a market system because most people have painters bid on jobs. This activates the competitive forces that make a market system what it is. Another exception is an operation on a large campus of over 5,000 resident students. A market of this size can usually sustain four or possibly even five competing campus businesses, but competitive businesses by definition invite certain headaches that monopolies don't. So, it might be more advisable to take a good idea and transfer it to another market or campus. Previously mentioned ideas are all proven, so trying them out in your town or school might be easier than you think. Remember that it's not the idea itself but what you make of it. You might think of a great twist to an old idea and double its potential, in which case you deserve as much credit as the person with the original idea, if not more.

An example of this is Mike Glickman of San Fernando, California. Mike took the idea of real estate listings and established the Phenomenal Distribution Company, which distributes real estate listings in the Los Angeles area. Real estate listings are not usually thought of as a particularly sexy or new breakthrough in business marketing. However, that doesn't mean that ideas such as these can't be made "successfully sexy." By the time Mike was 19 he had over 30 employees and had sold his concept in 65 cities in the United States and Canada. Now Mike has sold over $4 million worth of property and, at the age of 21, serves as an excellent example that an idea is only as good as the person who implements it.

Another reason not to compete head-to-head in a small market is economies of scale. This means that through doing things in a large fashion you can economize on certain expenses and even get your products a little more cheaply— by buying in bulk and getting a quantity discount. Because you don't have a large established business, you can't save on overhead since some expenses (such as a phone or business cards) are spread over a small number of sales in the early going. That means that you have to either charge more for your service or product, or be willing to sustain a loss until you build up your market share. Sometimes the competition can make that early loss a little bigger than you might have originally expected.

Jay Garnett, the pizza man, is a good case in point, except that in this instance he was the established business reckoning with the new competitor. When Jay started expanding to other colleges, he began to order substantially larger numbers of pizzas from the pizza shop he was dealing with. The volume increased, and so the cost per pizza to Jay dropped steadily as the pizza shop proprietor realized what a valuable customer Jay was turning out to be. At first the price was $1.25, then $1.10; finally Jay had his cost jammed down as low as 99 cents per pizza. In addition, Jay wasn't incurring that much extra overhead for each college he added to his pizza empire, so now his profit margin was nice and fat. Another enterprising type saw Jay making all this money hand-over-fist and decided it was high time someone else got in on the pizza windfall. The new competitor naturally started paying top price for his pizzas as well as all the overhead that goes with starting a new business. When Jay saw this coming, he lowered his price to prepare for the competition. All of a sudden this guy found his profit margin shortened from both ends. His costs were high and his sales price was lower than he had originally expected. Thus it was impossible to make the profit margin he had counted on to get his business off the ground. Unwilling to invest any money to hold himself up until he got a comfortable share of the market, he packed it in. Who knows, a few hundred dollars put in a massive advertising blitz might have boosted his sales to a profitable point, but we'll never know. In effect, what Jay had done was to erect a barrier to entry to the pizza delivery business in the form of low prices. This underscores the importance of using an idea that is new to the market you are entering. A person who is already in a market has too many advantages in being able to erect a formidable barrier to entry such as lowering price, increasing advertising to create customer loyalty, or tying up distribution channels. This doesn't mean you can't use an idea someone else has already used, but don't actively look for someone to compete against.

COST STRUCTURE

	JAY (1,500 pizzas)		COMPETITOR (600 pizzas)	
	Total	Per pizza	Total	Per pizza
Weekly overhead (phone, salaries, stationery, etc.)	$ 150	$ .10	$ 80	$ .13
Commissions (.25 per)	375	.25	150	.25
Cost of goods sold (pizza)	1,485	.99	750	1.25
TOTAL	$2,010	$1.34	$980	$1.63*

* Note that Jay can sell his pizza at $1.50 and still show a 16-cent profit, whereas his competitor must sell at $1.63 or take a loss. Obviously Jay can afford to keep his price at $1.50 and wait it out until his competitor either gives up or jams up his volume to get a better quantity discount on his pizza to lower his price. What would you do if you were the competitor?

The exception to this rule is people who are willing to put some money into their startup that will serve to hold them over during the first few months of business when losses are most likely to be incurred. However, the person who does this obviously runs the risk of losing the whole investment if he or she doesn't make it or decides to throw in the towel before reaching a break-even status. It takes a great deal of courage to stay in business while you are sustaining losses even if you see hope in the future. Doubts begin to set in, and all of your sanity says to get out, but for one reason or another you see enough hope to stay in. However, the difficulty of the situation is compounded by the fact that the best business people are the ones who know *when* to get out. Of course, you only hear of the success stories, the ones who stuck it out for ten years and who, like Ray Kroc, have a McDonald's to show for it. Never mind those people who stuck it out with dreams of ending up with a success like McDonald's

GETTING AN IDEA

but instead got a bankrupt catastrophe. The adage about not investing more than you can afford is applicable here. Remember that part of the objective of a student business is to learn and to develop some skills to facilitate the job search process. Later in this book there is a discussion of risk/return trade-off, which is relevant to the type of decision involved here. The purpose of owning a student business is to learn and to make money. If this is your first business, there are easier ways to make a buck while learning than cutthroat competition.

Many people might feel that not supporting competition on this level is tantamount to committing an act of blasphemy against the American work ethic. "Competition, it's what makes this country great," one bank in Boston, Massachusetts, advertises. I concur wholeheartedly, but I also feel that this particular philosophy applies to a market economy that exists in the country as a whole. However, in a college campus or summer business, a market economy does not exist on the same terms as we know it. In particular there aren't a whole lot of people running little enterprises similar to what you're doing, influencing supply and demand. Moreover, the campus market itself is somewhat limited and just doesn't support multiples of the same business. Instead, there is only you, and you in turn are influenced by the market system that operates around you in the form of local merchants. You indirectly compete against them, but you do not actually operate within their system. On campus you have a somewhat captive market away from their immediate competition. However, should you price yourself too high, that captive market could quickly escape as it becomes economically worth their while to make the trip into town.

Since one of the purposes of owning a small business like the ones I'm talking about is to make money, there is no reason to scare away newcomers with the prospect of startup losses. That will come later. Since success breeds interest, let kids who start businesses experience a little success—call it positive reinforcement—before they go head-to-head in a cutthroat competitive battle. The store in town offers enough competition without having to dig for campus market share

27

against your friends. There is a time and a place for competition in business, but it should not be when you're 18 and trying out your first venture. After all, there are enough ideas to go around. Like what?

Some Never-Used Ideas

Here are a few ideas that I have never tried, but I always wondered what might have happened if there had been time. They aren't guaranteed to make a million dollars, but it wouldn't be surprising at all if a few panned out. You be the judge.

Wake-Up Service

Lower-level college courses are notorious for starting at 8:15 A.M. If someone offered a telephone wake-up service, it seems to me, many students would gladly subscribe. Some of my buddies at school concurred, but for one reason or another there never was enough time to give this idea more than a casual thought. Having a class early in the morning is nothing short of a royal pain in the butt. Straggling in 10 minutes late, looking like a complete mess, is indeed a very rude way to greet the day. I happen to be one of those people who turn off the alarm clock, roll over, and go back to sleep, so this experience happened more than once (does this sound familiar?).

A ringing phone is one of the most obnoxious of all the sounds there are, and you can't just turn it off. You actually have to think when you answer a phone, and getting the cobwebs out of your brain is three-quarters of getting up. Just suppose you could get 150 students to sign up for $1.50 per week; you would be collecting $225. If you hired two people to do the calling at $6 each per school day (for what would amount to roughly 45 minutes of work), your labor cost would be $60. The phone could be gotten for a basic monthly charge of approximately $30 or less, depending on where you are. Two phones would be $60 per month, which works out to approximately $15 per week. (Note: It may be cheaper to hire students who already have phones with unlimited monthly usage and pay them a slightly higher hourly rate.)

Let's assume you had overhead of 20 percent of gross revenues; this would be an additional $60 per week. It would include things like advertising, promotion, stationery if you want, and other things that come up that you never think of. Thus your weekly income statement would look like this:

Revenues		$225
Less expenses:		
Labor	$60	
Phones	15	
Overhead	60	
Total		135
Profit		$ 90

A profit of $90 per week multiplied by 12 weeks in a school term equals $1,080 per term. That's not too shoddy, considering that you aren't doing any of the work except organizing the people who make the calls in the mornings. Now I'm sure that there are a few hidden snags, but even if you get half of what I'm estimating it still isn't too bad in relation to the time you need to put in.

Airport Taxi

Another idea was an airport taxi service during vacations, for colleges that are near an airport. Taxis are so expensive that if you could group people together, you would be able to charge each person less than an individual taxi fare but still make more than the individual fare a cab driver would make. The key is to get more than one person in each run. Obviously, you would have to limit your business hours to days immediately preceding and following school vacations.

Let's throw some numbers around to see just how feasible this is. Assume you could get an average of three people for each trip to the airport. Also assume that the airport is 15 miles away and a single cab fare is $20 (which is what the cab fare was to my college). If you were to charge each person

$8 for a one-way trip, you would gross $24 per trip. Your expenses are mileage (20 cents × approximately 30 miles = $6) and labor. Since you are driving, you can write off $10 for your own labor services to yourself. This leaves $8 profit for one hour of work. In addition, you have supplied yourself with work in the form of driving, from which you derived an additional $10 for a total in-your-pocket net of $18. Not bad for an hour. You will want to check, however, whether your insurance policy covers this situation and whether you need a chauffeur's license.

Don't let rising transportation costs scare you. It may well cost you more than 20 cents a mile to run your car. Remember, if it costs you more than 20 cents, it also costs a cab company more, and its price goes up correspondingly as does yours. It is all relative until cab companies find a way to run their cars more cheaply that you don't have access to.

Cigarette Subscription Service

Many students smoke a pack of cigarettes a day and would appreciate a service that supplied them with that pack every day in their school mailbox. Since newspaper subscription services may already use this distribution method, you could engage one of them to stuff subscribers' mailboxes with cigarettes. Someone with the newspaper service would know the mailroom setup better than you. If some customers smoked only half a pack a day, you would merely deliver their packs on odd days of the week. The selling points to the customer would be dependable service (our vending service was anything but), matches (our machines didn't supply those, either), and, most importantly, a competitive price.

Let's see how the numbers add up. Assume you could get 100 students and that you could get your cigarettes for 75 cents per pack by ordering in bulk. Vending prices are at least $1, so if you sold the packs for 90 cents, you would still offer a savings to the students. One hundred subscribers at 90 cents equal revenues of $90 per day. Your cost is $75 (100 × 75 cents/pack), so you have a margin of $15 per day. If you paid someone $6 to stuff mailboxes for 45 minutes, you would have $9 per day for profit and overhead. This results in a $45 weekly margin that fluctuates with the volume of customers you generate. If you went to a larger school and got 250 customers, your weekly margin would become $113. Once again, this is a good deal, considering you aren't doing any of the actual work. Dependability would be the key, along with a willingness to endure a slow first semester in anticipation of a strong following semester because of increased recognition and an established reputation. Remember that cigarettes are taxed by the states, and somewhere along the line you may find yourself submitting taxes back to the state, which could be a bureaucratic mess. But you'll never know unless you try!

Room Furnishings

A very simple idea that crossed my mind was a business that would sell room accessories. Black lights, colorful posters, or those simulated wave tanks that tilt back and forth are all the types of products I'm thinking of. Additionally, you could offer a line of curtains and small rugs. Set up displays in places of high student traffic that would also allow the students time to examine the merchandise. The mailroom and the cafeteria are two good places to start. Freshmen are always on the lookout for anything that might liven up their very dull rooms. Limit the number of products to a manageable few. The more partners, the more products. Everyone could take one particular area. The success of a venture such as this would be entirely contingent upon a successful marketing strategy, which will be examined at a later point in the book.

Bus Service

A friend of the family suggested at a dinner party a fascinating idea for a student business. (You'd be amazed at the ideas that come out of small talk at parties!) This friend had started his own shipping company in the very competitive New York City shipping area. He described an idea that had emerged from a college bus service. Many students do not own cars and need a convenient means to get into a town or city. This applies to colleges that are near large cities, such as schools in the metropolitan Boston, Chicago, or San Francisco areas. Perhaps this idea is a little more ambitious than some of the others, but his whole strategy revolved around obtaining the use of buses at a relatively modest price, enabling him to charge passengers a low fare. By planning to pay overtime to the bus drivers, he made his plan attractive to the bus company management or municipal transportation department. Why? One of the points that frequently comes up in union negotiations is overtime and how much overtime each driver can expect; management could offer 30 to 40 hours of overtime to drivers when discussing contract negotiations. The bus hours could be Friday and Saturday nights, with the last bus leaving town for the college campus 15 minutes after the last bar closed. The schedule would coincide with the hours a regular bus driver usually has off, making for an overtime schedule that would work beautifully. The service would attract both students without cars and those who find operating a motor vehicle prohibitively expensive. Moreover, with recent attention being given to drunk driving, you might find warm approval from the college administration. In addition, by encouraging mass transit—which is fast becoming a means of achieving the national objective of cutting down our dependence on foreign oil—you might very well receive encouragement and possible aid from local and state governments.

The point here is that you have to stretch your imagination a little bit. You have to analyze constantly in terms of "need perceptions." Once you have this attitude, the business world is yours. Go for it!

This has been an extremely difficult chapter to write, because it proposes to teach you something that can't be taught. Everybody has his or her own way, and mine might be right or wrong for you, but at least it gives you one perspective. If there is any one concept you should have learned, it is that the idea itself is fine, but what really matters is what you do with it. Possibly one or more of the ideas outlined here might interest you enough to look at it a little more in depth.

Finally, don't bite off more than you can chew. Start small and learn the ropes and pitfalls while the risk is low. Then start your expansion strategy. And try to avoid a head-to-head competitive battle with anyone until you have the resources (experience and capital) to hold your own.

The Plan
A. is the beginning of any business the first thing to deal

CHAPTER 3

The Business Plan

Let's assume that by one means or another you have come up with an idea that has all the makings of being the greatest thing since the food processor. The next part can be most important, depending on the complexity of your venture. If you are going into a business that involves anticipated sales over $1,000, it is very important to write a business plan. Writing a business plan is absolutely essential for anyone who is serious about starting a growth-oriented business with significant potential. Business plans accomplish several things that you, as the owner, need to do. Not the least of these is putting your ideas down on paper in order to organize your thoughts a little more clearly. If you have ever wondered why teachers frequently ask their students to write papers and essays, it is for this same reason—to get them to organize their thoughts more concisely.

For example, when I originally started toying around with the thought of writing this book, I really didn't know what form it would take or how I would approach it. All I really knew was that I wanted to write on the subject of young people getting involved in the free enterprise system, and I felt that there might be a market for a book on this subject. After trying it out on a few people with more than spectacular responses, I decided to see what it looked like on paper. It was about three days before I finally came up with a cohesive outline and a chapter breakdown that in its own way served as the business plan for this book that I later sent to publishers. That one three-day session is the nucleus of this book. A few ideas did get revised further or switched around, but the main structure has remained the same. When I was writing, I constantly referred back to my outline, which, toward the last chapter, was beginning to look pretty tired. The more I began to organize my thoughts, the more ideas started to surface about the book, and the more convinced I became that this was a marketable idea. In writing the outline, I started to get pumped up as an idea began to come to life. The more I thought about it, the more I devoted my spare time to writing down ideas for various chapters. And of course the more time spent on it, the less likely I was to throw in the towel on the whole project, since wasting time on a job I don't eventually finish is not in my nature.

A business plan works the same way. First you get your idea. As you begin refining it, you start jotting things down. During this phase, new ideas and approaches take shape, and the idea begins to take form and come to life. The more you start thinking about it and writing down things that will form the nucleus of the business, the more enthusiastic you will become as a dream approaches reality. As the idea becomes more and more realistic, you begin to realize that you do in fact have a marketable idea that can make you money and add to your credibility.

What Is a Business Plan?

A business plan has two purposes. The first purpose is to provide an organized outline of your proposed venture; the second purpose is to convince prospective investors that you do, in fact, have a viable project worth investing in. Generally speaking, the less of your own money you put into your business, the better. Most student businesses don't need investment capital anyway, but this will be discussed later.

A business plan is a written document that takes an idea, organizes it, refines it, provides objectives, and contains some market research to back up your contention that a future is possible for your company. Additionally, it lays out a strategy, defines the ownership breakdown if there are partners, anticipates problems, gives some indication of future sales and profits, and, finally, provides insight about the long-term future if things should blossom in a better-than-expected fashion. Business plans can be hundreds of pages long. You should see some of the business plans that the large multinational corporations put together when deciding whether to start a new division or enter a new market. In those cases, the investor they are trying to interest is upper management itself, who decides what operations get funded and which don't. However, a business plan for the campus entrepreneur usually needs to be no more than a few pages, including only the bare essentials. A minimal amount of time should be spent on elaborate market research, since that would use up the money and time you need to get the venture off the ground.

Writing a business plan is in many ways an education in itself. Not only must you be able to write clearly and cohesively; you must also know what you're going to be doing. Writing down your idea is just the beginning. Then you must work through a plan and anticipate problems. In the process, you start to learn about business and various business relationships. By playing the devil's advocate and looking for problems, you may find all sorts of pitfalls inherent in the type of business you want to start. In essence, what you are trying to do is familiarize yourself with the business you will be starting before you have started it. That way, you will encounter fewer surprises. Keep a sense of balance, however. Don't let a good opportunity slip away by overpreparing and overwriting your business plan so that it becomes a boring piece of non-pertinent information. On the other hand, don't do too little preparation and fall flat on your face.

Objectives

Start by defining your idea, and then put forth a set of objectives for it. In these objectives, list some of the things you wish to accomplish and the time frames in which to do them. Objectives serve as a rudder by which you steer your business. Objectives should also clearly answer the question of what business you are in. They are not set in stone and can always be revised later on, as is often the case. But with too much change the objectives will fail to serve their purpose. You don't want to be like a ship constantly changing directions, and not going anywhere at all. A review of objectives at the end of each semester is usually sufficient for a small- to medium-sized campus business.

A friend at Babson, Duncan Ross, had a landscaping business that he operated in Wellesley, Massachusetts. As the business grew, he set forth new objectives once or twice a year. For instance, he once wanted to expand his business into a surrounding town and, at the same time, improve his position in the towns where he already operated. Additionally, he wanted to increase his gardening contracts. His objectives were:

1. To attain a foothold in other towns and have eight to ten more regular weekly customers in six weeks by offering competitive prices.

2. To add one to two new customers a week in present markets for ten weeks through an aggressive sales and pricing effort.

3. To increase billings for gardening services by at least 10 percent per month for three months by a combination of new business acquired through door-to-door sales and increased referral incentives to present customers.

With these three objectives, Duncan determined the direction of his business for an entire spring/summer season. Those objectives told him where he was going to go and when he could expect to be there. They also helped him to define where he was going to expand, how much he should expand, and by when. Additionally, they described the strategy by which he planned to implement his objectives. Objectives should be kept somewhat general with only a few specifics, or they become too confining. These specifics usually show when an objective can be realistically achieved. For example, "To increase sales by 30 percent by the end of the school term" would be a realistic objective.

Strategies

Your objectives set goals that you try to attain; the strategies tell how you intend to achieve those goals. Duncan, in the example just given, had his strategy carefully set in after each objective. One objective was to increase billings on his gardening services by 30 percent. The strategy set after it clearly laid out a plan in which Duncan gave discounts to customers who had referred him to someone else. Moreover, Duncan planned to have the neighborhoods canvassed in search of even more new business. Your strategy should either be directly stated within your objectives or implied, so that you have an idea of what your approach to problems will be. In addition, you should have a section specifically on strategy, with a paragraph or two describing the strategy you have chosen and why you think it may work. This is a most important part of the business plan because it shows exactly what approach you are taking to penetrate the market. Your approach will have great bearing on your success.

There are two opposite goals that a business owner must decide between that have a direct bearing on the strategy he or she chooses. One of these goals is to capture market share (increase sales); the other is to increase the return on your investment (maximize profits). While this may appear to be an either-or choice, there is a middle ground. Basically, if you choose to maximize your return on your investment, you want to put as little as possible in the way of dollars and time back into your business. Obviously, the more you put back into your business, the less you will be able to put into your pocket.

However, if you elect to go after market share, you are then going to try to increase your sales not only on your own campus but also on neighboring campuses. To do that you need to implement marketing programs such as advertising, loss leaders (giving your product away at a loss the first time to attract customers who might buy other products at full price), and hiring salesmen, among other things. You'll be dipping into your profits to pay for these activities, but the market share approach increases the value of a business, in case you have plans to sell the entire business at a profit.

On the other hand, you may simply want to gain from the experience of running a moderate-to-large business in order to increase your attractiveness to future employers. There is also a small number of students who intend to run their businesses full-time when they get out of school, and are preparing themselves so that when that day arrives they already have the momentum. But one of the big problems with an all-out market-share goal is the time frame in which you have to work—a semester to four years. You simply may not have the resources, in time or money, to pull it off in so short a period.

Now, as I said earlier, this is not a black or white issue. You can elect to take a happy medium and increase market share by taking a moderate share of your profits and putting it back into the business. In order to grow, your business does need money. Sometimes you can internally finance your growth by generating enough profits so that you can meet your own cash needs. Sometimes you need to borrow money to finance your growth. Even if you don't do extensive marketing, two items will gobble up cash very quickly for growing businesses.

One is accounts receivable: those people to whom you give credit. If you want to see your business grow, you're going to have to extend credit to some of your bigger customers merely to secure their business. Offering credit is a marketing tool, used to convince people that they should do business with you and not someone else. The other item that requires cash is inventory, unless you operate a service business. The higher the volume of business you do, the more inventory you need to keep. If people have to wait for you to run to your distributor rather than pick your product off the shelf, they will eventually give their business to someone else who can meet their needs more quickly.

Jason, who had the keg delivery service, provides an excellent example of someone who elected to go after market share without realizing that there was a cost associated with growth. As Jason's sales began to grow, he found that the various student government associations, which usually ordered large quantities, had to operate on credit because the school needed time to process checks. Fraternities, also regular customers, demanded credit. This meant that Jason needed two weeks' worth of cash to cover these orders, which amounted to roughly $1,200—not a small piece of change for a sophomore. What's more, in order to keep the fraternities' business, he needed a constant supply of four or five kegs on campus because frats are known for throwing a pledge night party on the spur of the moment and need kegs right away. Not to keep an inventory would have meant risking having the frats go to a local liquor store for their party and talking to the liquor store owner who might try to counteroffer Jason's deal. So, although the practice was costly, Jason decided to carry inventory and extend credit. The result was that his strategy of capturing market share paid off. His business ended up doing an annual volume of $30,000 and eventually, when he graduated, he was able to sell the business off for $4,000. Jason not only got invaluable experience, he also made a substantial amount of money. Jason's experience was considered unusual enough that he got accepted at every graduate business or management school he applied to, including Harvard and Yale, and he is now one of my classmates at Yale.

One last benefit of writing out your strategy is that you may very well find an unexpected flaw hidden in your initial plan.

A real estate investor in New Hampshire, in anticipation of the land and housing boom, bought two acres of land with plans to build a house on each acre. His strategy was to buy the land, start building, and sell his half-built houses a few years later at double the initial cost. On the surface, his plan made plenty of sense. Land prices were then rising rapidly. He figured he could make $40,000 to $50,000 in all. After much talking and running around, he began to break ground. Unfortunately, he had never checked with the local zoning board, and much to his chagrin he discovered that the land was not zoned for residential buildings. Oddly, he had the rest of the project figured out to a T, with all sorts of net present values and discounted cash flow projections. If it hadn't been for that zoning blunder, he might actually have made all that money in his otherwise flawless plan.

Donny Heap, of Duxbury, Massachusetts, also decided to build a house, but he included a little room for error in his plan. Donny bought some land in New Hampshire with the idea of building to sell. The one deviation in his scheme was the method of building. Donny's strategy was to enlist the help of his fraternity brothers to build the house in return for letting the frat have the use of the house for over two years. Donny had to pay out-of-pocket only for materials; the labor was free. Consequently, because of his reduced need for money, the return on his investment was much higher than it might have been. When, at 22, Donny graduated from college, he was the proud owner of a house that had a market value in excess of $60,000. There aren't many 22-year-olds who can make that claim.

Policies

Now that you've considered objectives and strategies, the next thing to include in your business plan is a short section on the policies of the firm. In a strategic planning class, I heard an analogy of a business as a ship, the objectives as the destination of the ship, the strategy as the rudder, and the policies as the banks of a river, which served as guidelines to the achievement of a goal or objective. If that got lost in the translation, let me say it in plain English: policies are some of the guidelines that you set up within your organization. This, in turn, guides the strategy, which, in turn, fulfills an objective.

A friend of mine from Michigan, Jack Weddington, provides a good example of why you need to set policies. Jack started a wholesale clothing business selling directly to stores. When Jack started the business, he set a policy that directed its sales efforts. Jack's policy was to sell to a store no matter what the discount was, so long as the net selling price was no less than his actual unit cost. This led to a very aggressive sales force that generally got the merchandise into the stores they wanted. This, in turn, reinforced Jack's initial strategy of gaining quick credibility by putting the goods onto store shelves as fast as possible. By being able to say that he had a Bloomingdale's or a Brooks Brothers store as a customer, Jack had the acceptance he needed to offset his young age; he was 21. Thus, Jack had a policy that implemented his initial strategy. The policy was the tool to get the strategy into effect. The strategy, in turn, was fulfilling one of Jack's objectives, which was "to become a viable force in the industry within 18 months."

There is another side to the coin, however. You should

be aware of the danger of having too many policies or too inflexible a set of them. When you first start out with your venture, you will probably be new to the game. Keep your policies very general and flexible at first, and tighten them up as you go along and begin to understand the market you are in.

A good example of this is the publishing business I started with my roommate Jim Tabner. When we came out with our first edition of *Shot,* a college soccer magazine, we decided to set some policies on the flexibility of our advertising rates. Instead of deciding on a fixed number of dollars per page of advertising, we opted for a looser, less restricting policy of maximizing the revenue per page.

This policy sounded very vague, and it was. It was also fortunate for us because, as things turned out, we acquired quite a few accounts that originally paid us only a fraction of the stated rate. However, in forthcoming years most of them stayed on with us and eventually paid full price. Once you have an advertiser, there is an excellent chance of keeping the account. Eventually the advertiser will pay the full tariff.

Policies should never be so tight that they fail to let you adjust to a given situation. The small business environment is always changing, and the small business owner must be able to adjust to a changing situation. Ability to change quickly is one of the advantages of small business over big business. For instance, if you have a policy of not selling your product or service at a loss and a prospective customer comes to you with an enormous order, half of which must be sold to him at a small loss in order to beat the competition, what do you do? About 95 percent of the time, you would reject the order for fear of letting the situation get out of hand. However, there will be a few instances in which you may detect a host of more profitable orders in the near future from the same customer, and you may decide that a small initial loss is worth the potential sales and profits that are around the corner.

During my junior year in college, I had a wholesale/retail bumper sticker business called Collegiate Slogan Stickers. I approached the purchasing agent for a company that owned a string of college bookstores with the proposition of making up individual bumper stickers for each school, as well as selling him two lines of preprinted bumper stickers that said "Tennis is my Racquet." At that time we had a policy of not selling any products at a loss. This shrewd buyer was insistent about lowering my price. Eventually I sold him the tennis bumper stickers at a loss on the condition that he buy some custom bumper stickers, which had higher profit margins anyway. The net result? An overall profit of a couple of hundred dollars, despite the small loss we sustained on the preprinted bumper stickers. The icing on the cake was that we later got an offer to bid on a contract for 10,000 bumper stickers for the Massachusetts state college system through a referral by this fellow. We were the low bidder and won the contract. This is a case in which a policy or rule was stretched a little bit to adjust for the circumstances, so we eventually ended up with several thousand dollars in sales as well as respectable profits. If that policy had never been stretched, we would have gone home empty-handed.

Don't go overboard on stretching policies. Your partners won't know when to stretch policies and when not to. This defeats the purpose of having policies in the first place. Moreover, your customers may get a little riled if the word gets out that you are bending the rules for some and not for others. This just serves to undermine your credibility. You are walking a fine line between too much compromise on policies and not enough. The decision, finally, is yours; that is half the fun of owning your own campus business. The experience you get by making these kinds of decisions simply can't be bought at any price. Three years of having to make decisions like those just mentioned, day in and day out, gave me several years' worth of experience over my classmates. This experience, I'm convinced, was a significant factor in getting my first job offer from Boeing and eventually being accepted at The Yale School of Management.

Plans

Plans are a fourth vital element in the designing of your enterprise on paper after objectives, strategy, and policies. Plans are the immediate steps you will take to implement your strategy and fulfill your objectives. In other words, what are you going to do *now?* First, keep in mind that plans must fall within policy guidelines. (One exception is long-range planning, which extends over several years and is more closely identified with strategy. Long-range planning will be discussed later in the chapter.) A student business should rarely have plans covering more than one semester, and the best planning is usually done on a monthly basis, since those are the time increments by which a semester is broken.

Scott Johnson, of Andover, Massachusetts, is an example of a good planner, most probably because planning was so essential to his business. Scott bought an existing rug business that served colleges in and around New England. Scott's business, Reasonable Rugs, sold rugs at the beginning of each semester (and during the semester when he felt like it) to college students. At each school, Scott would set up a huge display representing the inventory he had on hand. No preliminary advertising was done. Scott relied primarily on his displays, usually featuring bright, attractive colors that couldn't help but catch the eye of a passerby. Before each semester, Scott would plan out day by day the colleges where he intended to display his wares. In addition, Scott would plan when he hoped to have each administration's approval, when he would arrive, where he would display, and when he would leave. Sometimes he was forced to move on, because of his precise schedule, before he was satisfied that a college had been fully penetrated. So, to be safe, he left one afternoon a week open for return trips. The way Scott figured it, the key was in maximizing every available amount of time into product display in the first two weeks. Scott's reasons were twofold. First, wallets and pocketbooks are full when students return from vacation, especially summer vacation, when kids usually have disposable income to spend on their room environment, be it rugs, lamps, or a stereo. Second, most students characteristically make 90 percent of the changes or additions to their rooms in the first two weeks of the semester. If they don't make any changes in the first two weeks, they usually won't—they get lazy and just plain comfortable with what they've already got. Scott, realizing all this, made planning a key strength of his company. He had his two-week sales blitzes planned out to the last detail. And it worked! In one school year, which was about five weeks of campus rug displays, Reasonable Rugs grossed over $15,000.

For Scott, planning showed itself to be the key. Although some other enterprises do not rely quite as heavily on planning, it does play an integral part of the running of any firm.

Partnerships

Taking on a partner in a student business is to your advantage. When you are attempting to start a business during college, one of your most valuable and limited resources is time. Time is one thing that you need to start an enterprise, but it's not a commodity that you can buy more of. There are only 24 hours in a day, and there is nothing you can do about it. What's more, a large chunk of this precious resource is spent on studying. When you add sleep, classes, meals, and a few hours of relaxation, you are left with between three and five hours a day to run your business. If you take on a partner, this time allotment doubles, and so should the potential of the business. You could, of course, elect to hire employees to retain 100 percent equity, but this just increases financial requirements in the early stages when sales can't justify the additional labor costs. A partner is free labor, since he or she is more than willing to donate time free of charge in return for the ownership of a budding enterprise. Taking on a partner either gives your business significant amounts of potential or allows you to spend less time running a profitable business and have time to cover your other needs. Sometimes it can do both, depending on the goals of the individual partners and whether they want free time or a dynamically growing business.

A partner can also be a motivation factor. For me this has always been an important reason. It's so easy to get up in the morning with several business-related errands to do and say, "What a hangover; I'll do them tomorrow." Not so when you have a partner who is pulling his or her weight and expects you to do the same. There are always times in running a student business when you question whether the whole thing is worth it. Even the most successful business owner will reach down moments, and having a partner who can pick up the slack and encourage you in these times can save you from throwing in the towel when you will almost surely live to regret it months, or even years, later.

Bob Ritter, from Poughkeepsie, New York, was a typical campus entrepreneur who sold off a thriving enterprise and regretted it. In his sophomore year at the University of Texas, Bob had a variety of small ventures, such as refrigerator rentals and travel tours, that gave him a healthy amount of pocket money. Bob had a chance to sell his businesses to two enterprising freshmen for a hearty sum, a temptation few can resist. A year later I talked to Bob, who confided that he had been looking around for "something to sink my teeth into" ever since. Bob's problem was that he didn't have a partner telling him that his business was a bud about to blossom. Moreover, Bob was used to the prestige of being the campus operator as well as having more things to do than there are hours in a day. He was very much like the corporate executive who retires after years of being in the business jungle and finds that retirement isn't so great after all.

Financial considerations and the size and scope of your prospective business may indicate the need for partners. The larger the business, the larger the risk. If you are going to attempt to begin your business career by starting a 50-college pizza delivery service, you'll have a lot to lose if things go poorly. A partner cuts your personal losses to whatever portion of the business he or she owns. A partner who owns half the business is responsible for half of the losses as well as the gains. A general rule of thumb is that the higher the risk of failure and the more you have to lose, the more partners you should take on to spread the risk around. However, if you have the stomach to accept a loss of several thousand dollars before you have even graduated from college, by all means keep as much as possible for yourself. More on this subject in the next chapter.

If you have decided to take on a partner, it is very important that you have your partnership explicitly defined in your business plan. This is important for even the most Lilliputian of enterprises, because when and if the pie gets bigger, each partner naturally wants a larger slice of the action; defining this at an early stage can save you headaches as well as friendships.

Dealing with a partner in a day-to-day business relationship can add considerably to your own personal growth. A partnership is often exposed to strains that ordinary personal relationships are not. You will learn earlier than most people the benefits of modifying your wants to become more of a "give and take" kind of person. In any partnership, there are times when you and your partner will be on opposite sides of the fence on a particular question. Both you and your partner will be called upon to compromise and modify your positions. Mature business executives do not throw up their arms and stomp out the door when a decision does not go entirely their way; a student business owner cannot run a successful enterprise with actions like these either. Unfortunately, a lot of promising ideas never get off the ground because partners cannot modify their personal opinions. Eventually these people must learn to adapt to decisions that they may not personally endorse, or their business careers are limited before they even start. A business partnership lets you see just how good you are at dealing with people in general, and this facet can enhance your attractiveness to future employers.

My experience with Jim Tabner in our publishing business is especially pertinent. Much of the credit for the early success of our venture goes to Jim, as the original idea was his. Nonetheless, as partners we often had our differences. Both of us have stubborn streaks that run true and deep. As success hit our young publishing firm, it was imperative that we learn to compromise in our decision making and understand that neither of us could have our way all the time, a process that came to both of us none too easily. However, a year later we had both learned to compromise peacefully and leave our differences behind after a final decision had been made. Both of us now are considerably easier to deal with. This kind of compatibility in business is what separates the team players from the disruptive loners in the real world.

Market Research

The next step in your business plan is to include some market research, defining what your target market is and how you intend to reach it and stating why you feel that there is a market for your goods or services. Market research can be as sophisticated as formal surveys and computer modeling or as casual as questioning various friends and associates. Just remember that your objective is to back up your belief that a future exists for your idea. This is important not only to would-be investors but also to potential partners.

Good market research surveys the environment to identify where the competition will come from, as well as consumer attitudes about an idea. It is important that you not overdo market research and waste precious resources such as time and money on unnecessary research. The amount of market research should be correlated to the size of your startup and to the amount of money you wish to raise from outside investors.

Financing

You've got objectives and a strategy that you think will get you where you want to go, and you have laid out your partnership plans and how the pie is going to be sliced up. You also have a few policies that you intend to follow and some market research to back up your convictions. Now what you need is a financial analysis that shows there is indeed a buck to be made.

Sometimes when you start out in a small venture, financing is necessary to get you and your business off the ground. The majority of student business startups do not require financing, but yours may be the exception that does. After you decide what your cash needs will be, the next step is figuring out how you expect to meet them. You can elect to supply all the money necessary yourself or borrow from your parents or even from a friend. You should include this subject in your business plan. Probably most important, you need to determine how much income you need to cover these costs.

Financial analyses can be very complicated and tricky, but on the level at which you will probably operate, they can be simple and straightforward. Included in your analysis should be expected costs and overhead and a rough idea of how much income will safely cover all costs. The best way to approach this is to create three scenarios. The first is to take a lowball approach and see where you would stand if things went poorly. Exactly how much money would you (or your investors) stand to lose? Next, take an educated guess at what you actually expect sales and related costs to be. Last, take a highball approach and see what would happen if things went beyond your expectations.

When you look at all three of these projections, you can get a rough idea of the upper and lower limits of what you stand to make or lose. This is called sensitivity analysis. How sensitive are your costs to a 10-percent drop in revenues, a 20-percent increase, and so on? In Chapter 8 there is a discussion of how to set up projected earnings (Pro Forma) statements as well as how to figure out expected costs.

Long-Range Plans

There is one last piece that you need to include in your business plan—future long-range plans. For a student business this usually means six months to a year later, whereas for a major corporation long-range planning encompasses five- and ten-year plans. However, it is all relative to the size and scope of the business in question. If you are graduating in a year, the long-range plan may be to beef up your market share and sell your business at a healthy profit. However, if you are looking at two or three more years of school, long-range plans might include expanding until finally you subdivide accounts into on-campus, other campuses, and non-campus markets. Knowing that this is what you are going to want to do in a year can help you form policies and objectives now, which will facilitate the transformation process.

Financial Statements

A financial statement gives prospective investors and partners a feel for what kind of profits can be expected if all goes well. Various accounting statements, such as an income statement and a balance sheet, are discussed in the chapter on accounting. You need them to show people the profit potential for your company. These statements generally should be the last section of your business plan.

Summary

By now you should have a good idea of the first step to transforming your idea into reality by putting it down on paper. As I said earlier, it is often unnecessary to write out a long, detailed plan on a campus venture, but the bigger the undertaking, the more time and effort should go into your business plan. It took five weeks to write the 26-page business plan for my soccer magazine. However, to start a simple laundry pickup business you obviously don't need anything that elaborate. You should have, however, at least a two- or three-page business plan containing your objectives, strategies, plans, and financial forecasts. You may find that what looked like a great idea on the outside is beset with inherent problems that make the undertaking impractical.

A Summary of the Business Plan

I. Objectives
   A. What business am I in?
   B. What are the goals of the venture?
   C. What strategies will be used to achieve them?

  D. Where am I going to be in . . .
    1. One month?
    2. One semester?
    3. One year?

II. Strategy
  A. What is my central strategy? How does it fulfill my objectives?
  B. Why will it work?
  C. Am I concentrating on market share or increased profits or a combination?

III. Policies
  A. What are they and why are they being implemented?
  B. How flexible will they be?

IV. Plans
  A. What immediate actions are to be taken to implement my objectives?

V. Ownership plans: Should a partnership be considered?
  A. Why?
  B. How? Who gets what and what do they do in return for their piece of the action?

VI. Market research
  A. Target market
  B. Environment

VII. Financing
  A. Cash needs now and later
  B. Descriptions of how I came up with the figures I did
  C. How cash will be raised

VIII. Future Plans
  A. What are they?
  B. What will I be doing *now* so as to meet them more easily?

IX. Financial Analysis
  A. Projected sales and costs
  B. Breakdown of costs: Can any fat be trimmed?
  C. How much income is needed to break even, and when will that event take place?

FORMING STRATEGY AND PLANS

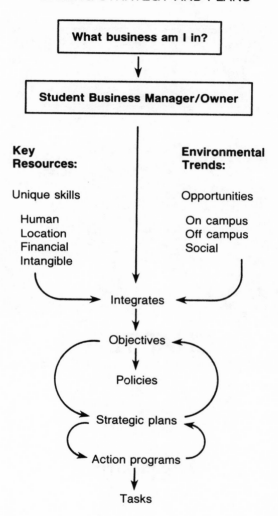

Adapted from David C. D. Rogers, *Business Policy and Planning* (Engle-wood Cliffs, NJ: Prentice-Hall, 1977). Used with permission.

CHAPTER 4

Marketing

Of all the aspects of running a business, one of the most important is the design and implementation of an effective marketing plan. Marketing encompasses all the actions necessary to get a product or service sold. The marketing person takes the finished product and puts it in the hands of the consumer. This involves establishing a method of distribution, setting a proper price, promoting it through advertising or other means, and finally determining what new needs the market has in order to come out with more new products on a timely basis. After all this is done, it is time to go out there and sell it. Because it is such an important part of marketing, selling is addressed in another chapter.

You have to have sales to keep your business alive, and marketing directly controls the selling effort. Some products are sold to the buyer over the counter, in which case you want to stimulate customer demand through advertising promotion; other products are sold by a sales force to a select targeted market. All advertising or selling is targeted in some way, so you must carefully plan your marketing strategy and which prospects within your market you or your sales representatives will call upon to utilize their time most effectively.

You might make mistakes in your accounting methods, and you can even afford a few financial errors, but if the marketing effort fails no one has anywhere to go. After all, without any sales, how can the accountant make any entries? How can the finance person project cash flows if no sales have been made to provide historical data? The gaining of hands-on, practical, grass-roots marketing experience is one of the most valuable parts of running a student business. Even if you do not go into a marketing-oriented profession, you still will know how it works and how to make it work for you.

Marketing is dynamic. It changes and, insofar as you must be doing something right if the product is selling, it is measurable. A decision to market a product at a 10-percent lower price can have some visible results within a month. A great deal of strategizing takes place in a marketing effort. You as the marketer have to think of the combination of steps you will take to get your potential customers to buy your product.

This chapter breaks marketing down into the various components over which you have control. In addition to explaining each of the components, the chapter explores the optimum mix of them so that they form a cohesive marketing plan within a strong overall strategy. As usual, there are examples of student business marketing to show that, yes, it can be done.

The Four P's

The components of your marketing strategy should be as simple as possible when you start out. The following is a discussion of the four P's, which are the backbone of any marketing strategy: (1) Product, (2) Place, (3) Price, and (4) Promotion. The combination of these four elements will make up your marketing strategy or market mix. Each of these components will be discussed at length before the market mix.

Product

Without a product you have nothing. The product can be a service or an actual object, but in the end the product is what the customer receives from you for parting with his or her hard-earned money. Choosing the right product for a student market, or adding a product to your product line, requires a combination of creativity, common sense *backed up* by concrete reasons you think your idea can work, instinct, and luck.

This may seem like an odd combination, but to start you need some creativity to think of something new and/or different that you feel will sell. Common sense backing your idea keeps you from implementing weird ideas that will ruin you financially when they fail. Thus, with common sense and a creative imagination you should develop some reasonable ideas suitable for the marketplace. Instinct enters into the picture at this point because you must have a conviction that this idea is damn well going to work. Finally, you need a little luck on your side, as do we all, to get you over the rough spots.

Creativity, intuition, . . . and luck. A little creativity will do wonders for even the blandest of products. Just look at Gary Dahl, who invented the pet rock. Who in his or her right mind would buy something like a rock when any old field has hundreds of them for free? However, add a little pizzazz and imagination to the marketing, jazz up the packaging, and bingo, you've got the potential for a catchy product like the pet rock. A fraternity had the idea of putting together fruit baskets and selling them at exam time for $9.95.—a simple idea with a creative touch that made the product itself unique. Plain old fruit probably wouldn't have yielded much in sales, but fruit baskets targeted toward exam week were quite successful.

A creative product will catch the eye of prospective buyers. Once you have their attention, you can explain the features and benefits. If your product is totally uncreative, you are fighting an uphill battle to get your customers' attention. A high emphasis should be placed on creativity, since it's always nice to be unique. People who sell such mundane things as tableware or ball bearings deserve our sympathy. What on earth makes one brand of ball bearing different from another brand? But getting people honestly excited about a creative product is considerably simplified.

Intuition is an intangible that really can't be taught. Either you get a good feeling about an idea or you don't. I am a great believer in my gut feelings or instincts, but some people prefer more methodical ways to substantiate their belief that their idea has a future. These people will research the dickens out of an idea before they decide to take the plunge. Actually, market research is valuable, and I do use it to back up my convictions, but too much planning for your product can take valuable time away from the implementation of your whole game plan, slowing down the learning curve that takes place during every new product introduction. And too little research into the acceptance level of your product can expose you to unnecessary risk. Don't fall prey to the problem of being overly production-oriented at the risk of forfeiting your perspective on the target market. Rather, the most commonsense way of getting confirmation of your gut feeling about the potential success of your product is to think it out thoroughly and then do a little investigative legwork. Talk to potential customers to see if they would buy or not, and take it one step further to find out why or why not. Make a call to some neighboring schools to find out if anyone is currently providing a similar service, and if so what the acceptance rate has been among students. If not, then *voilà!* You have discovered an untapped market. Be careful, though; sometimes a product can be a perfect fit for one market but a mediocre or less than successful product in another.

A good example of this is the beer industry. Often a beer can be a regional favorite but in another area have severe difficulty penetrating the market. Schaefer beer, for example, has a wide acceptance in the New York City area, but it has not penetrated the New England market to the same extent. Likewise, with my refrigerator rental business I often found one campus could be a virtual gold mine, while other campuses barely took notice of my marketing efforts.

Usually when you start your business, you offer one product or service, and it is usually a hit-or-miss proposition. If that one product or service doesn't catch on, you don't have any others to fall back upon to keep the doors open. Because of this, it is important to make sure that you have tried to get as much of a feel as possible for how the market will react to your product without dragging on the implementation of your business into eternity.

There is another factor in choosing a product for your marketing mode, one over which you have no control—the element of luck. Don't let anyone tell you that business success, whether on the campus or in the real world, is due purely to skill. Success and failure in business always have an element of luck.

I knew a guy whose business was delivering snacks such as cheeses, wines, imported beers, and other yum-yums to the doors of students on campus who had called in their orders. Mike, the proprietor, had sunk considerable money into expanding his business and product line. However, after the state legislature suddenly raised the drinking age, the college revoked Mike's right to operate on campus because of their concern about his delivering liquor to underage students. Their concern was based on the fear that the college could be exposed to legal action if a minor were to purchase liquor from Mike and then go wild. This is a perfect example of how luck can work against you.

While Mike's experience shows how luck can foul up even the best-laid plans, the reverse is also true. Luck can make some businesses succeed in spite of themselves. Being in the right place at the right time is critical to the success of a product or business. Refer back to the beer industry for an example. Light beers are very popular now, but did you know that light beers were test-marketed years earlier with disastrous results? A great idea but at the wrong time. There isn't a whole lot you can do about luck, but be aware that timing and luck do play a factor in your success, and do everything in your power to stack the odds in your favor. Leave as little as possible to chance, and its negative effects will be minimized. Again, do not overreact and become obsessed with looking for bugs under every single little stone on your path. Avoid too much elaborate market research that chews up considerable amounts of your time and money. Just remember that chance is a factor in success and make it work with you and not against you. Be thorough but not overly meticulous.

Expanding your product line. Once you have introduced your first product, you may wish to expand your product line, or you may have introduced more than one product when you started your firm. When you offer more than one product, you have what is known as a product mix. Your products should complement each other, as when one product serves to draw customers to buy another product or when they fill a gaping hole in a line of products.

For example, if you knew of a particular shoe store that carried only one size of shoe, in one style, you might not be inclined to waste your time going to the store unless you knew for sure that you liked that style and that the size it carried was yours. However, if that shoe store expanded its product line to carry all sizes, you would be more inclined to stop by to see the selection. This is what is meant by filling out a product line. If the shoe store were to add shoe polish to its product line, it would be complementing its current product line. After the customer had bought a pair of shoes, the salesperson might suggest a can of shoe polish to keep the new clodhoppers in shape, and presto—a bonus sale. The shoes drew in the customer, and the final result was not one sale but two. Remember that every time you add a product to your product line you need to look at your business plan, ask, "What business am I in?" and see if the added product is consistent with your original objectives. You may need to make some changes. In the example, the shoe store might change its objective from "We are in the business of providing quality *shoes* to the public" to "We are in the *foot care* business and provide to the public footwear and all accessories that relate to foot care."

Expanding your product line is one of the most effective ways to make your business grow and increase your sales. Duncan Donahue's coupon booklet business (see page 139) put him in the advertising business, since a merchant who buys a place in the coupon book is, in effect, advertising. Ultimately, Duncan decided to expand his product line and began to publish, in addition to his coupon booklet, maps of local towns with advertising on the borders. Duncan acquired the actual town map from the city hall and then sold two sizes of advertising on the border of the maps. He printed several thousand maps and then he left them in stacks around town on the counters of all his advertisers, as well as in other high-traffic areas such as banks, supermarkets, and the post office. The various banks, stores, and supermarkets gave the maps to the public free as a service. The public benefited by getting free maps, the advertisers benefited by gaining access to a rather unique media vehicle, and, best of all, Duncan made out by earning a great deal of pocket money. By expanding his product line, Duncan was no longer dependent on one publication, his coupon booklet. As a result, he doubled his revenues and profits.

Another successful product expansion example involves John Soncar, who operated a beer machine. Of course, this kind of business is not recommended because of its illegality, but it does illustrate quite nicely how an expanded product line can increase business and profits. John had originally placed his beer machine (a soda machine stocked with beer) in an out-of-the-way room in the cellar of a dormitory. The machine released a can of beer after 35 cents had been deposited, which resulted in a profit of 10 cents per can. John had all five selections for the machine stocked with beer, until he noticed that there was no soda machine in the dorm. After doing some quick calculations, John concluded that a can of soda would yield a profit of 15 cents per can or a 50-percent increase over a can of beer, which had a profit of 10 cents. So he increased his volume and profit by replacing two beer selections with soda selections. John had doubled his market. Before, when all five selections gave beer, customers were given a wider selection; but if one of those selections was not available, the average student would usually select another brand even if it wasn't the first choice. However, soda customers who found no soda would rarely switch to beer. Rather, they would walk to the snack bar. When John expanded his business to reach the soda-drinking market, he doubled the use of his machine by the dorm.

When you start thinking about expanding your product line, look for resources your current products have that your planned products can also utilize. Your current product line may have an already existing loyal customer base, which is a resource, as in the case of the beer machine. This same customer base may also be an excellent prospect for your new product. This means you would not have to incur massive extra selling costs. The existing customer base is already being served, and thus salespeople do not have to be increased to reach any more of your market.

Loss leaders.   Sometimes a firm elects to give away or sell an item at a reduced cost to draw you in the door so that you will buy its more profitable products. These items are often called "loss leaders." Have you ever wondered how safety razor companies can afford to give away so many of their razors in those special deals? Although I'm sure they're great guys, the people who conceptualize those offerings don't do it to keep America shaven at lower prices. They do it because if they give you a razor, guess what you've got to buy. You got it: razor blades. By giving you a razor at, say, a loss of 50 cents, they have in return acquired a lifelong customer for their razor blades. In this example, the expanded product line makes perfect sense, because both products serve the exact same market as well as complement each other. The previous example about the beer machine also showed a situation in which products complemented each other.

In short, when you are contemplating an addition to your product line, you must always look for something that complements your existing product line and/or uses an already existing resource. Products can complement each other by more than just being similar. For instance, a fellow who had two boating marinas opted to complement his product line by starting several auto muffler shops. On the surface, boating marinas don't seem to complement a car muffler shop, but they do. In times of prosperity boating marinas are usually prosperous as well. However, in times of economic downturn marinas don't do so well, but auto muffler shops are always busy. People would rather fix up the old heap rather than sell it and get a new one per the American dream. So this man always had a prosperous business no matter how the economy performed. It was a rather clever way of complementing his product line.

Place

The placing of your product or service involves all of those aspects connected with the distribution, possession, and timing of your product in order to satisfy customers. You might have the greatest ski boot in the world, but if you distribute it through bathing suit shops in the summertime, what chance do you have for success? Little or none. However, if you place it in retail shops specializing in ski wear and accessories in the late fall, you have complemented a good product with a sound placement strategy.

Your objective should be to reach the widest possible segment of the student body if you have a non-specialized product or service that is targeted at the general student body. To do this, you must have a proper place for display, and you need to discover a time when the greatest number of students will be exposed to it. Three ideal locations to present your product or service, applicable to virtually all educational institutions, are the cafeteria, the mailroom, and the book store.

The cafeteria. Almost every student must pass through the cafeteria or dining hall doors several times a week, and more times than not they must wait in slow-moving lines, which is ideal for you. If you have a line of students in front of your display, you have a captive audience. Assuming that you are presenting a salable product, you must take advantage of this fact. Drop an attractive blanket or cloth over a table to give a pleasant and more professional air to your operation. In addition, a large cardboard sign (3 by 5 feet or so) with your promotional message gives the public an idea of what you're peddling. (A little creativity here will help.) The purpose of the cardboard sign is to get your customers' initial attention; after that it's up to you to draw them in until they sign the order or make the purchase. Leave a stack of business cards out so that if you haven't completely sold the students on your wares by the time they have passed your table, they at least know how to get in touch with you if they have a change of heart. Finally, if possible you should have samples of your product on the table for display. There is nothing better than a product that sells itself; if you've got one, by all means let the world see it. If you are dealing with a service, have some printed literature that customers can take with them, giving a complete breakdown of what is provided, how much it costs, and where and how to order. If you do all of these things, you will have a successful display table, and barring poor service or a poor product, sales should begin to roll.

The mailroom. An additional place to present one's goods is the mailroom, through which virtually all students pass several times a day. A mailroom does not have the captive

63

audience that the dining hall does, but it offers the same high volume of student traffic. If your school does not have a mailroom, the locker area where students keep their books is an excellent alternative. The advice about setting up a table is applicable here; the only real difference is the location.

Wholesaling to the book store. The book store works best if you are selling a product rather than a service. If you sell to the book store, you become a wholesaler, since you are not selling to the end consumer. There are two things to keep in mind when considering the book store as a distribution outlet. One is that you are competing for the attention of the public with a host of other products, most of which are made by companies that put a considerable amount of time and effort into packaging so they'll catch the eye of the customer. Consequently, you should have either a unique product or an attractively packaged one.

The second thing to keep in mind is that in order for the book store to consider taking on your product or products, you in turn must offer something, namely, room for a 50- to 100-percent markup. That means if you sell your product to the store for one dollar, the store is going to want to sell it for anywhere from $1.50 to $2. That spread is what they pocket for giving you the shelf space, providing exposure of your product to the general public, and covering their own overhead and profits. The magic question is, will your product be affordable after the retailer (the book store) has added on the markup? Don't forget you too want to make some money on the deal, so basically you are looking for something that you can buy or make for about 25 percent of what the final selling price will be. Double your cost to cover your overhead and profit, then double that for the bookstore's markup. You can see why your cost has to be about one-quarter of the final selling price.

Let me give you a real-life example with my bumper sticker business, which was marketed through college book stores. Since we were attempting to reach a wide range of colleges and universities, individual booths or tables were out of the question; I couldn't be at all of these schools at once. College book stores thus were the way to go. I figured that the highest an individual bumper sticker could sell for was $1.50. That meant that, with the book store taking a 100-percent markup, my selling price to the book store could be no more than 75 cents. Further, working backward, I figured my expenses could total no more than 40 cents per sticker (after all, I had to make some profit). Figuring my marketing and selling expenses would be equal to roughly 10 cents per unit, I arrived at the fact that my direct cost per bumper sticker had to be no more than 30 cents. That is how I approached prospective printers with my deal. Give me custom-made bumper stickers at 30 cents per unit with a reasonable delivery time, and you'll have my business. All our calculations were based on a high-quantity turnover, which, thankfully, we made, or we would have been sunk.

One thing to remember is that your role in these three distribution methods involving the cafeteria, the mailroom, and the book store are different. In the first two your role is one of a retailer, and your objective is to please the public. In selling to the book store you are becoming a wholesaler, and your objective is to keep the book store managers happy. If they aren't happy they won't place more orders with you. Remember the two ways you can keep the managers happy: give them room for a good markup and a product that will turn over frequently, which means high sales. This justifies the shelf space they have given you.

Price

Along with choosing your product line and placing it, the marketing plan involves pricing. Pricing can be a strategy unto itself and very often is, but for now we will keep things simple.

If your price is too high, you will eliminate a portion of your potential market because they cannot, or are unwilling to, pay that sum in exchange for what you are offering. If, on the other hand, you price extremely aggressively, or low, you may have so much demand that you cannot possibly satisfy it all.

Ideally, you should peg your price at a level that optimizes both consumer demand for your product and your profits. If you sell out too fast, you know you could have made more money if you were a little more patient and set a higher price. It might have taken more time to sell your product, but you would surely have made higher revenues and profits.

The flip side of the coin is pricing too high. If you do this, you may find yourself with few or no sales. This can be compounded in a school environment, in which you may have also gotten a reputation for being a greedy, profit-crazy capitalist pig. If a reputation like this gets out of hand, people stop considering your products and look elsewhere for a better buy. Even though you may have dropped your price, it doesn't matter, because they don't even bother looking at your prices anymore. The way around this is never to price something so as to be considered exorbitant. There is usually someone who sells the same product for more, so when possible give advertising comparisons that are in your favor.

Overall, however, avoid the temptation to price high in the student market because students are by nature price-sensitive creatures and tend to look for a bargain. The time when a pricing decision is hardest to judge is when you are offering something new that is not available anywhere else—you have cornered the market. This is most likely to take place with a service-oriented business, because it is unlikely you will come up with very many products that you alone have the capability to manufacture or provide. Thus, if you conceive of a service that seems to have virtually no direct competition, how do you price it?

It is my feeling, contrary to fundamental marketing thought, that in such a case you price it low and give it maximum exposure to the campus to let students realize how great it really is. Once you think you've hooked them, slowly start raising that price. If you don't raise it too quickly and scare them away, you should eventually get a strong customer base at a profitable price.

If you choose to go after the bucks and set your prices high, more power to you; have fun spending your profits. However, if someone comes out with an equally good product or service for a lower price and takes all your customers away, that's the price you pay (no pun intended) for taking the high-price risk. If someone sees you making a fistful of bucks and thinks he or she can do as good a job at a better price, that person probably will. The beauty of the market system is that you can charge whatever you want and no one is going to stop you . . . but neither is anyone going to help you if you set yourself up for competition.

The key factors affecting your price are cost and risk. Your cost tells you the very least you can charge for a product or service. The risk is how high you can set your prices without losing all your customers. The lower you can drive down direct costs and overhead, the better price you can offer or the more money you can make. This means going to your suppliers and negotiating a lower price. Once you get a profitable business going, there are two advantages of having your suppliers rebid on your business. First, you get a chance to see how competitive they are in the price they give you. Second, you get a feel for just how badly they want your business in terms of providing more service. Suppliers are not going to give you a price break out of the goodness of their hearts. You are the one who has to initiate matters. Don't try to ram it down their throats, either, or else a defensive reaction is inevitable. Some casual hints about how their closest competitors gave you a price break and *really* want your business often are sufficient to arouse their competitive instinct. The lower you can get those costs, the more flexibility you have in pricing decisions; and that ultimately gives you more control over your own destiny, which is one of the reasons you started a business anyway.

Promotion

Once you've got your product and have selected the proper distribution place at the right price, promotion is the final step. It serves to let the public know what you're offering and how to get it. Promotion includes person-to-person sales efforts, advertising, and all other actions taken to promote your products or services.

There are as many possibilities for successful promotion

as there are fish in the sea. Raffles, direct mail campaigns, clever packaging, and matchbooks with your logo on them are all ways of letting the public know that you've got something that they should have. Business cards are a form of promotion. Free samples to the first 50 customers seldom fail to draw a response (unless you're giving away something totally bizarre like toilet plungers). Freebies and discounts are extremely effective for the college market, because students are so money-conscious. Few people will turn down something that's free. If you offer two-for-one deals, discounts, and other "deals," you will surely get your student market to give your product or service a good long look with an eye to buying. However, don't give away freebies if you are marketing a non-repeat-purchase product. The point of "deals" is to arouse enough interest that the customer comes back for seconds, thirds, fourths, and so on. But you've got to have a good product for this strategy to work.

At one college, pizza delivery businesses became the rave venture to get into because they can be quite lucrative. One creative student ran an advertisement that, from a promotional point of view, was brilliant. Here's a facsimile of the caption:

FREE SEX!

Well, not really. But now that we have your attention, we would like to tell you about a discount XYZ Pizza is offering. So, if you wait for our delivery man you will get a 50¢ reduction in our plain pizza price with this coupon.

Because of the competition in the pizza business, this owner had decided to go after market share and forgo profits for a while. He decided to have a sale, but with so many pizza businesses in the marketplace, the problem was how to let the public know. His ad, which he placed in the college newspaper, certainly got everyone's attention. Problems resulted when competitors began to honor his coupons, thus defeating their purpose, the result was that competitors lowered their prices by 50 cents to match his coupon offer. Nonetheless, this is a great example of how promotion works and what it is meant to do.

There's also the tale about another beer machine that I came across as a teenager. Although the actual operation was illegal, it is an excellent example of how *creativity* can be used effectively in a promotional effort. Sam was 19, and for some unexplainable reason, he went out and bought a soda machine for $600. He put the machine in the cellar of his college dormitory and filled it with soda. The results were encouraging, but Sam still didn't think he was getting as much out of his investment as he thought possible. A short while later he heard of a soda machine stocked with beer instead of soda, located on another college campus. A week later his five selections were filled with beer. Business went up sharply, but then dipped and eventually leveled off as the habitants got used to the novelty of having a mechanical beer-tender. Then Sam hit upon his brainstorm. Having filled all his selections with medium- to top-shelf beer (Bud, Miller, Schlitz), he took out one selection and replaced it with the cheapest beer he could find that yielded 40 percent more profit. However, he put "surprise" Michelobs (a top-shelf brand) in at every fourth or sixth spot and changed the vending selection to read "Surprise Michelobs." Apparently, the dorm's gambling instincts were aroused, because that sucker sold out in a day. The next day the same thing happened. The final result: sales went up by over 25 percent, and the profit margin widened substantially.

The importance of promotion is magnified by the fact that at this point you probably have already invested amounts of time and money in product, place, and price decisions that you don't want to see go down the tubes. Compounding this is the fact that, at the beginning of your new venture, you must make a name for your business out in the marketplace. You are starting from scratch and need to inform your potential customers about both your firm and its products or services.

Advertising.   Probably the most widely used method of promotion is advertising. An advertisement is a message, and how good a given advertisement is depends on just how effectively that particular message gets across to the targeted audience. There are two components to good advertising: one is to select the proper medium to carry your message; the other is to present your advertising message in a manner that will attract the attention of potential customers and persuade them to buy.

In the student market there is a narrow choice of advertising media. Student-run newspapers, a school radio station, athletic game programs, and homemade mimeographed advertisements are all common conveyances for student-oriented advertisements. You may very well wish to use a combination of vehicles, but this is largely dependent upon the budget you have for your advertising effort. In any case, there are several questions you must answer in order to select the proper medium:

- What kind of audience does the medium reach?
- How expensive is it?
- How many people are reached per dollar?
- What is the attention span of the audience when listening to or reading your message?
- How much flexibility do you have with your advertisement? (For instance, some athletic programs will let you place only one ad for an entire season.)

Effective advertising is not a one-shot effort but rather a concert of strategic placements over a given period of time. There are very few one-shot advertisements that get a good response. To place one ad and expect the world to come knocking at your door is not realistic. Opening up with a rapid-fire advertising blitz is more likely to elicit some response. In the end, a carefully selected range of advertising vehicles that follow a planned strategy, with possibly one getting more placements than the rest, is the most effective way to launch a student business advertising campaign. For instance, you might place one ad in the campus newspaper for the whole campus and one ad in the town newspaper, and put up posters (written in different languages in the foreign students' lounge). Just be sure that you have a reason for where and why you advertise. Don't do it simply for the sake of doing it.

What your written ad looks like has a bearing on its effectiveness. Your message should be simple and direct. If you can be creative, by all means do so. Study ads of similar products or services in local and national media and try to see just what the advertisers had in mind when they designed the ads. You should avoid using humor, though, because it distracts from the message. Who cares if the audience laughed when they saw your ad, if they didn't get the inclination to buy? Some of the most humorous and award-winning advertisements made were done for Alka-Seltzer. But most people don't know that the advertising agency that designed those ads got fired because sales never took off and even began to dip. Learn from that lesson and stick to selling your product.

It is also not wise to include too many ideas in one ad, as the reader can often get confused. If you have a couple of main themes, split them up into several ads and then perhaps make only one ad that includes them all.

Large ads, no smaller than a quarter page and up to a full page, depending on the expense, are best. The bigger the message(s), the bigger the ad should be, especially if you are presenting several messages at once. Let's face it, no more than a quarter of the readership of almost any publication reads the small ads; so small ads are often an exercise in futility. Why spend advertising dollars unless you're going to get a bang for your buck? My philosophy is, if you're going to spend money on advertising, make sure your ads will be seen.

You might also wish to include some graphics or a photo in your ad. Purely verbal advertisements tend to scare readers away, as we humans are basically a lazy lot. If people think they are going to have to read a whole ad, top to bottom, before they understand what the message is, they will in all likelihood just skip it and go on to the next page. However, put something like a good-looking model in a bathing suit in your ad and see how many people skip your ad. But then they wouldn't see your message, because the model would be distracting. So the key is to put something visual in the ad that will have some relevance to your advertisement.

The ideal advertising campaign comprises three or four means of advertising, two of which are targeted toward the hard-core base of potential buyers. The other two advertising vehicles should reach the general public and might be the student newspaper or color mimeographed sheets posted around the halls (with permission, of course). The advertising campaign might be split into halves. The first half tells why everyone should switch to or *start buying* your product or service, with a high degree of emphasis on price, since students are especially sensitive to that. It also tells what is new about the product, why it is worth the cost, and other features and benefits you wish to stress. The second half of the campaign tells the public why to *keep buying* your product and might be more comparative in nature. This half shows why other competitors (vaguely referred to, but never by name) are not as good as your product and service. The ads should include some visual aids and should be pleasing to the eye.

This is really just brushing the surface, because advertising is such a broad subject that whole books have been written on the subject. However, in advertising to the student market one needs to know less about the more sophisticated methods and just use more plain common sense.

But barring a dramatic overnight leap in demand, how will you know if your ad campaign is working? One of the hardest things to accept when dealing with the components of marketing as individual segments is that they are extremely hard to measure precisely, especially in the campus business environment. If you advertise in the college newspaper, it is unlikely that demand for your product will shoot up right away. Rather, it takes effect over time and builds up a steady base of customers. For many people, this can be frustrating, but if anyone had a magic gimmick that would jump sales 30 percent tomorrow, he or she would be foolish not to sell this formula to the nation's largest companies. One way to get a feeling for how the public perceives your company is to do market surveys. However, these are not always accurate and can often be misleading, especially when one is surveying students. Students often take such questionnaires lightly and answer them exactly as they *don't* feel, thus defeating the purpose.

Talking with friends and customers you run into can give a pretty good picture of how your marketing effort is doing and where you may be missing the boat. Use the opportunity to ask someone what he or she thought of the advertisement you placed in last week's newspaper. This is one of the best ways to measure your marketing effort. If you are the outgoing type and enjoy running your business enough to discuss it a couple of times a day with anyone and everyone, you are encouraged to do just that.

Many large companies prefer to use questionnaires, especially if they cater to a select group of customers rather than to the general public. Situations like this are applicable to some student businesses, too. For instance, if your business involves publishing, in which you sell advertising to produce revenue, you have a select group of customers—your advertisers. In these cases, a questionnaire can be effective in measuring how good a job you are doing in marketing your product. I recommend picking your top 25 customers and personally filling out the questionnaire with them. This adds the personal touch and also leaves minimal room for error in the event that they don't understand a particular question or don't feel inclined to answer it thoroughly.

A short note on using questionnaires is in order. Questionnaires can be a very effective tool; however, they can also provide you with misleading data if you ask the wrong questions the wrong way to the wrong people. Make sure you know what information you're after and design the questions accordingly; but be careful that your questions don't suffer from ambiguity. Also, it is vital that you target your questionnaire to the right people. Thus, if you're trying to find out why there isn't more market acceptance for your product or service, don't send your questionnaire to current customers, because they are already buying.

Ultimately, though, the only true measure of your marketing effort is your sales volume. Your price may be great and your advertisements may strike interest, but if people aren't buying, you aren't doing the job. If you aren't getting the business, there has to be a reason. Are you sure the need perception is there? What would it take to get *you* to buy? Would you buy your own product if you had no vested interest in its success? If you answer *no* to these questions, you have to overcome those obstacles that would keep you from buying.

In this brief discussion of measuring your marketing effort, we have seen just how difficult it is to calculate with any precision the effectiveness of any particular component of your marketing mix. However, the effectiveness of your overall plan is measured quite simply in sales. Some people have successful ventures and really never know why. They know that the overall plan works, but they don't really know what part or parts of it are the principal factors behind their success. You can take surveys, ask your friends and people you meet, and you will get a good feel for what people like and don't like about your product or service.

This should all be stored in the back of your mind until you feel that you must reformulate your market mix, and then these various inputs you have received should begin to influence your policy.

The market mix.   Integration of the four P's is what makes up the market mix, or strategy. They must be blended. It would make little sense to offer a product or service targeted to people in town and advertise it on campus, or vice versa. It would also be self-defeating to introduce a high-price product to cost-sensitive students without discounting it for a period of time. No one would initially buy the product, and consequently they would not realize the benefits that serve to bring repeat customers. It is unlikely that your product would ever get off the ground.

One thing to keep in mind, though, is that not all student businesses incorporate all of the four P's; those that do might not explore them all in any great detail, nor do they need to. Here, for example, are two businesses that approached marketing in different ways:

74

Carl was a fairly ambitious sophomore in college. During his sophomore year he started a disk jockey service using his very elaborate stereo. After a while the business caught on, and Carl upgraded his stereo equipment even more, along with his price. By the time he was two years out of college he was getting $300 a night for about four-and-a-half hours' work. This is a good example of a business that continued after graduation. Because there were no practical cash expenses except those Carl chose to incur in the form of new records, virtually all of this was pocketed as profit. The point of this story is that there was a minimum marketing effort behind the several thousand dollars that Carl pocketed. He did little promotion, no advertising, had no distribution channels (because, of course, he was a service business), and you would not call him inexpensively priced. But what Carl did have was the product, and he knew it. When people throw a party, they almost always pay a premium to ensure that everything will be a success. Consequently, Carl could get away with being a little more expensive than his competition. In addition to his minimal promotion, he had a product that benefited from word-of-mouth reputation and, because he played such good music, that in itself was a type of promotion. You can see, then, that you don't need to utilize actively all of the four P's for a successful marketing effort. Rather, a combination of one or two can often suffice, depending on the type of business.

On the other hand, some student businesses are large enough and profitable enough that they choose to put on a full-scale marketing effort actively utilizing each of the four P's. Our second example is Jason, who did a full-scale marketing program for his keg delivery business. He put advertisements in school newspapers as well as in other publications. He held raffles, did market surveys to learn his competitors' prices, constantly looked for ways to broaden his product line, and set up customer service programs. Jason chose to do much of this for pure marketing experience. It is extremely difficult to measure how much additional business he received as a result of his emphasis on marketing. However, one thing that can be measured is that in the two years he had that business, Jason lost only three accounts out of a base of over 60 (5 percent), which is not bad at all.

Jason and Carl differed in their approaches to marketing. Jason chose to give marketing significant emphasis. Carl put his resources into improving his product (one of the four P's) through upgrading his stereo equipment and buying the newest popular albums. But both needed to recognize the value of each variable, at least within reasonable bounds or ranges.

You have to take a long look at your product to see where the widest possible market for it is. Then you have to price it accordingly, and if it is highly priced but nonetheless an excellent product, you must discount it in order to make the public aware of how good it is. Thereafter, the product will sell itself. You must select a placement or distribution plan that reaches out to the largest number of people within your target market. If you've got the latest in punk leather jock-straps, you probably want to set up your booth in the gym. If, on the other hand, you are dealing in jewelry, the gym might not be best. A display in the women's dorm would be more appropriate for jewelry.

How you structure your market mix is your decision. For me, this is the most fun, because this is where imagination and creativity have no limits. If you succeed, which you probably will, the satisfaction you get is solely your own. If you haven't experienced this euphoria, go out and do it. I promise you won't be disappointed.

For Further Reading

The following short, concise, informative readings are available from HBS Case Services, Harvard Business School, Boston, MA 02163:

Borden, Neil. *Note on the Concept of the Marketing Mix.* Harvard Business School, 1960.

Corey, Raymond. *Marketing Strategy*. Harvard Business School, 1978.

Moult, William. *Advertising Copy Research*. Harvard Business School, 1979.

This memo is available from the Yale School of Management, Box 1A, New Haven, CT 06520:

Permut, Steve. *Management Memo: Some Things a Manager Ought to Know about Questionnaire Design and Use in Problem Solving*. Yale School of Management, 1980.

Here are two basic textbooks:

Govoni, Jeannet and Allen. *Marketing Problems—Cases for Analysis*. Columbus, OH: Grid Inc., 1977.

Michman, Ronald. *Marketing Channels*. Columbus, OH: Grid Inc., 1974.

CHAPTER 5

Selling

SELLING

"Salesmen acquire a particular selling skill
by constantly acting in a particular way."
—Anonymous

The Importance of Selling

Regardless of what field you enter in life, you constantly need to sell yourself, and this is a skill that can be taught. Even a job interview is merely an opportunity to sell yourself to your prospective employer. Prospective employers in turn are selling you on their company or department. After you have your job, there will be occasions when you have an idea, and whether or not it is accepted or rejected very often depends on how good a job you do in selling the idea to the decision makers. This applies not only to business folk but also to the journalist trying to persuade an editor to publish an article or a lawyer persuading a judge about the application of a point of law. Whatever the profession, there are times when you will wish to convince someone to accept your line of thinking, and this is the essence of selling.

Experience in selling is also important in that it sharpens your communication skills considerably. Communication is the heart of all interpersonal relationships, and unless you wish to be a hermit, you should constantly strive to improve these skills. Many studies have shown a direct correlation between success and the ability to communicate. Selling forces you to communicate, because how else can you show people that your product or service fits their need? To do this, you must listen in order to understand your customer's need and then respond to show how you can fill that need. These are the two parts to communication. Many people think that communication is merely the ability to talk well, but it is equally important to listen. It is very important to remember that when you talk, you teach, and when you listen, you learn!

Regardless of whether you intend to make a career in sales or not, you can only benefit by learning some of the ground rules of selling. It's important to understand selling skills so that you can better sell your ideas and yourself to those around you. The remainder of this chapter is split into two sections. The first discusses the concepts of the selling cycle and the various phases that make up that cycle. The second part tells about the various selling skills that you employ to achieve success in sales.

The Sales Cycle

Identifying and Qualifying Opportunities

There are three parts to the sales cycle. The first part, which can be called preparation, has two components: identifying opportunities and qualifying those opportunities. When you identify prospective opportunities, you are looking for people or companies that seem to have a need for your product or service. If you are selling refrigerators, for instance, you are looking for students who live on campus and wish to supplement their food needs because institutional food just doesn't make it. When you are identifying opportunities, you are searching for your targeted customer set.

Then comes a process of qualifying those opportunities. You should try to eliminate those prospects for whom chances of closing the sale are minuscule. This allows you to concentrate your efforts on those prospects whose chances of buying are higher. When qualifying, you are looking for a real or perceived need. If you have a prospect who appears interested in your goods, and who also has the ability to make a buy decision, that person is a qualified prospect. If you have someone who you are convinced has a need, even though that person may not initially recognize it, he or she is also a qualified prospect. However, if you have a dozen other prospects in this situation who are more receptive to the need for your product, you put those prospects who don't recognize their need at the bottom of your qualified list. The more the prospect fits your qualifications, the more resources (including time) you should commit to that prospect.

When I worked for Boeing in the Computer Services and Consulting Division, one of the most important things we had to identify was whether an interested prospective client actually had the authority to make the decision. In other words, we wanted to know whether we were dealing with a decision maker or, as was often the case, a recommender. If we were dealing with the recommender, we had to reach the decision maker and determine if he or she was in sync with us. If not, we exited as quickly as possible to spend our time more productively on more qualified prospects.

For example, working with the managers at General Dynamics on the implementation of some of Boeing's newest engineering technology, it appeared to me that all the right signs were there. The client had a real need, Boeing had some very sophisticated application technology that solved General Dynamics' need, and the managers were enthusiastically embracing our solution. However, I had not done a thorough enough job qualifying. Ultimately, as is often the case, the real decision maker was the guy holding the checkbook, and he felt that General Dynamics could get by just fine without Boeing. That lesson was paid for with a month of my work time.

Sales Activities

The second part of the sales cycle encompasses the sales activities you undertake to close the sale. First you plan the strategy you will use to make the sale. For example, if the buyer is price-conscious, you will emphasize your price if it is low or you will avoid the subject as much as possible if it is high.

Your strategy will vary from prospect to prospect, but in the final analysis it behooves you to set a strategy for closing the sale. To aid you in determining sound strategy, you should get as much background information on your prospect as possible. This will impress customers, since you will be able to demonstrate a genuine understanding of their needs. The next thing you need to do is to set specific objectives for your sales call. For anyone with a product that has a sales cycle of more than one sales call (generally speaking, products that sell for high dollars need more selling time), a logical objective is to stimulate enough interest so that a follow-up appointment is gained to continue the sales cycle. By knowing what your objectives are, you know exactly what you want to discuss. If you seem disorganized and unprepared, you reduce your credibility in the eyes of the prospect.

The last part of your sales activities is making an effective sales call in order to get a commitment from your prospect, whether it's an actual commitment to buy or a commitment for another appointment. This includes dressing professionally, being prepared, and being sensitive to your prospect's needs (that is, not being pushy if it creates an uncomfortable atmosphere).

For those of you whose projects will involve mass merchandising, there is a different angle to what I've just discussed. Mass merchandising refers to those who are setting up a table or booth in the dining hall or mailroom, where product turnover is expected to be high. The first objective should be merely to get people to come to your booth to take a look at what you've got. A strategy here might be to serve free glasses of wine to anyone who comes to your booth during dinner hour to attract prospects. The principal effort in this situation revolves around your point-of-purchase sales promotion, whether it is a sign, billboard, or demonstration. Whatever you elect, remember that your strategy should focus on how you are going to get people to come to your booth.

A good example of this is the Boston Chipyard, started in Newport Beach, California. Founded in 1976 by Mike Hurwitz, 16, brother Mitch, 13, and Frank Beaver, 13, the Chipyard sells fresh chocolate-chip cookies. Sales of the cookies have boomed beyond expectation, with sales in the millions of dollars and outlets from California to Boston. Originally started as a good way to save money for college, the venture has done a good deal more than that.

The way the Chipyard gets you to come to its booth is simple. They bake the cookies right near the counter. So, if the aroma isn't enough to snag you, the sight of rows and rows of soft, chewy chocolate-chip cookies certainly is. (Unfortunately for my girth, it has lured me on numerous occasions.)

This example shows that age is not a barrier to business success, and in fact can be helpful, because younger people are often more open-minded than their elders.

Closing

When you determine that the sales cycle has progressed so far that, if the prospect doesn't sign now, he or she never will, it is time to close the sale. However, the closing portion of the sales cycle can be preempted by the prospect's giving you an obvious buying signal.

But there are a helluva lot of people in this world who are downright indecisive, and these people will usually not give off any strong buying signals. You must ask these people for their order. You'd be surprised at how many will say yes so long as you don't come across as overly arrogant.

There are two times when it is best to try closing. One is when you detect strong buying signals from the customer, which might be statements of approval or need. Sometimes they can be expressed through body language, but however these signals are expressed, they convey the prospect's feeling of need or desire for your product or service. Of course the body language could be expressing *lack* of desire. While I was selling advertising space for our soccer magazine at Babson, a local merchant who was notoriously averse to college solicitors began breaking pencils while I was giving my sales pitch. Thirty seconds later I found myself being physically escorted to the door. You can't win 'em all! If your prospect does begin to agree with the benefits of your product, he or she is expressing a buying signal.

The second time that an attempt to close is appropriate is when you feel that you have done everything within your power to persuade the prospect that a need does exist for your product. To continue the sales cycle any longer would just be wasting the prospect's time as well as yours. There comes a time when you must call it a day and devote your efforts to other potential prospects. It is at this juncture that you ask for the order. If the prospect says no, just be thankful that at least you now know, and then spend your time on more productive matters. If the prospect says yes, you got what you were after and achieved your end objective—to make the sale.

Many people believe closing to be the most important part

83

of the sales cycle. Let's face it: it takes guts to ask someone for an order when you aren't sure whether you have convinced him or her yet. It also takes a lot of sensitivity to realize when someone is hinting to you, verbally or otherwise, that he or she will sign your order (or never will). Many good salespeople can perform the entire sales cycle to perfection, but when the time comes to close, the cat gets their tongue. The result is that they wasted all that time and effort, and there are few things worse than wasting time. If you use your time efficiently and effectively, you will stand a good chance of being a good seller of products, ideas, and yourself.

Selling Skills

Regardless of what you may have thought, selling *is* a science. There are techniques, used by sales professionals, that can greatly enhance the probabilities of your closing a sale. The techniques don't necessarily guarantee that you will close every sale, but they do mean that you will close 10 percent or so of those sales you might otherwise have lost. They increase the probabilities of your gaining business.

Selling is a game of numbers. If you knock on enough doors, you will find enough interested prospects. If you use the following skills, you *will* close business, unless you've got a really unusual product, such as a funeral service for dead flies, that makes people think, "Wow, is that kid weird!" However, assuming that you are as normal as the rest of us and have chosen something that has selling potential, you should learn to use these six basic selling skills: (1) general benefit statements, (2) probing, (3) summarizing, (4) support statements, (5) understanding and handling customer attitudes, and (6) closing.

General Benefit Statement

A general benefit statement tells how your product or service can be of help. Since you usually don't know specific customer needs at the beginning of a sales call, your benefit statement must be of a general nature. A good example might be: "Mr.

Advertiser, store owners all over town would like to get a sizable share of the high school business. The Carson's Advertising ledger offers a new way to reach those students in an effective way."

A good general benefit statement does two things. First, it describes an assumed general customer need, which you can detect by getting a little background information on your customer. In addition, it describes a general benefit that answers the assumed need. Obviously, the key to good general benefit statements is making the right assumption regarding a customer's general need. Therefore, you want to be rather vague so that you don't miss the boat and end up with a prospect telling you thank you, but he really doesn't have that assumed need, so there really isn't any purpose to be gained by discussing your product's benefits any further. To avoid this, you make an assumption that is so general that it is hard to be wrong. Things like improving profits, reducing costs, and improving business are all very general benefits. The better you think you know your customer, the more specific a benefit statement you can make. If you are talking to a Chrysler dealership in town, it would be safe to make a general benefit statement such as: "Ms. Dealer, many car dealers are feeling the pinch of imports and a decline in sales. My advertising brochure reaches each parent and gives the best exposure in town."

The purpose of a general benefit statement is to generate a customer's interest so that you have his or her attention when you get into the meat of your pitch. Greeting prospects with a canned pitch is not advisable because it sounds corny. However, not everyone can wing it, so it depends on your style. Practice ad-libbing general benefit statements, because if you don't get off to a good start and get your customer's attention, you face an uphill battle when you move on to the next step in the process—probing.

Probing

Probing is a process of asking questions to uncover customer needs. You probe with either open or closed statements, depending on the circumstances. Customer needs can be awfully hard to discover, and wide-open questions with no specific purpose generally don't get them uncovered. However, you have to get at those customer needs in order to make a truly effective pitch. If you don't know your prospect's specific needs, you are shooting in the dark. Sometimes you hit, but most of the time you don't. Probing helps you get more hits.

The open probe is an open-ended question that allows your prospect a great amount of latitude in his or her response. By using open probes at the beginning of a sales call, you let the customer direct you to his or her problem. A typical open probe might be "What kind of problem do you have in your line of business, Mr. Customer?" This allows the customer to take the conversation in any direction. Open probes encourage a customer to talk freely on a given topic. They can also stimulate a customer to expand on something that may already have been stated. However, open probes don't always do the trick, as some prospects are uncommunicative. In these cases, shift gears and start using closed probes.

A closed probe is a specific question that steers the sales conversation to a topic of your choosing. If a prospect is uncommunicative, you must take charge and direct the conversation. Assuming that the example invoked during the discussion of open probes led to an unenlightening answer, a good example of a closed probe would be "Ms. Customer, do you think you're getting your fair share of student business?" The prospect has no choice but to address your question. If the customer is not getting his or her fair share of student business (have you ever heard of business owners who felt they were getting enough or too much business?), he or she is forced to voice these feelings or lie. Closed probes are an effective method of opening a prospect up about his or her needs if there is a tendency to be unresponsive.

Supporting

Through the use of open and closed probes you should have uncovered a variety of needs that your customer has. Whenever a prospect reveals a need, you support that need with a two-part support statement. The first part is to agree with the need in an understanding way: "Yes, Mr. Prospect, I can see that a problem like that might concern a business owner such as yourself." The second part of your support statement is to introduce the appropriate benefits your product or service has that can solve that need: "The Carson Memo Book solves that problem with the easy reference guide, thus making sure you don't forget appointments."

When a customer makes a favorable comment about your product or your company, reinforce that comment with an expanded agreement statement. "Ms. Customer, you're right: soccer is a good sport to advertise with and has met with wide acceptance by other merchants in town." You never want to let a positive statement go by without expanding on it so that your prospect becomes even more aware of the positive attributes of your product or company.

If, as often happens, the people you are selling to make a favorable remark about how good it is to see the young people of today taking on the challenge of starting a business, immediately agree with them. Tell them flat out that it isn't easy, and it's because of such people as themselves who believe in student enterprise that the whole thing is possible.

When my partner and I were doing the National Championship Soccer program for the NCAA, there was a one-week selling window from the time we were awarded the contract to the day when everything was due to the printer. I was climbing the walls trying to get everyone out generating advertising sales. It was about the third day of the week, and we were one ad short of reaching our break-even point, after which all additional sales would be pure profit. It was late in the afternoon and I called on one of the local hairdressers. Halfway through my pitch, the owner interrupted me and remarked how he missed his youth soccer days, and wasn't it great that soccer was catching on in this country. I wasn't about to let this opportunity pass by and came back with a support statement to the effect that I felt soccer was great, too, and that's why I was publishing the championship program. After all, I reasoned, if I were going after the big bucks,

I would have skipped soccer and done football programs. At that point he began to nod his head. Next move? A closed probe that closed the deal. I asked him if he thought it beneficial that students work their way through school. When he replied yes, I let him know that I was taking it one step further and starting my own business. Ten minutes later I was on my way home with a $300 check in my pocket for a half-page ad.

Summarizing

The ability to summarize can very often be a significant factor in closing a sale. At various points throughout a sales call your prospect will give you a valuable piece of information, such as identifying his needs or agreeing on the benefits of your product or service. At these points you should step aside from your sales pitch and summarize what he or she has told you. "So then, Mr. Customer, I understand what you have just said; you. . . ."

One reason for summarizing is to make sure that there is no misunderstanding of the discussion. Another benefit is that if you have a prospect who has agreed on most of your benefits, you can slowly begin to rope him or her into your corner. "Ms. Customer, you have said that you have need A and need B, and we have agreed that my product has benefits A and B that meet those needs. Is there any reason not to sign a contract now?" What else can the customer say? You've shown her that you understand her needs and that she has agreed on your benefits. That has all the ingredients of a sale. If the customer says no, then she must come up with a reason.

There might be a reasonable objection that you hadn't thought about before. Now that you know about this objection, you can address it and improve your chances of closing what might have been an unsuccessful sales attempt. Try to lay a foundation throughout the sales call, using summaries of the needs and agreements for the product benefits. If you do this, you will significantly improve your chances of a sale by reducing miscommunication and increasing prospect recognition and agreement.

SELLING

Dealing with Customer Attitudes

The four kinds of attitudes that you are most likely to encounter when you first meet with a prospect are acceptance, skepticism, indifference, and objection. A prospect either likes what you've got, is skeptical, couldn't care less, or objects. Let's go through each one of these attitudes and examine what to do.

There is only one thing to do when you have a prospect who likes what you've got, and that is to go for the close. Why argue with a person who is ready to buy? Believe it or not, many sales are lost because the salesperson tries to oversell. Halfway through the sales pitch, the customer starts to show some buying signals, but the salesperson is determined to finish the whole presentation. What happens? The prospect loses interest and decides not to buy.

During my sophomore year, when we entered the refrigerator rental market, I was canvassing one of the local colleges, Pine Manor, for rentals. I was giving my pitch to a young woman, and I could sense she was warming up to me. At one point she agreed how convenient it would be to have cold yogurt and milk so that she wouldn't have to go to the dining hall for breakfast. Did I give a support statement and go for the close? Of course not; I just kept babbling away about how marvelous it would be to have her own refrigerator and how even her next-door neighbor had one. What was that? Her next-door neighbor had one? The next thing I knew she was going across the hall to see if her next-door neighbor would let her use the fridge, and presto—a lost sale. If I had kept my trap shut and asked for the order when she was agreeing with me, I would have been $30 richer. However, we all learn from our mistakes. People make mistakes; fools make 'em twice!

When you find a customer who is showing signs of acceptance, that's the time to close, get the order signed, and get the hell out of there. More than one salesperson has been known to overstay his or her welcome; make sure that you don't.

One of the attitudes most frequently encountered is skepticism. Because you are a student and are relatively young, you will run into this much more frequently than a professional salesperson.

Believe me, when encountering a skeptical prospect, it's not uncommon to get tongue-tied and lose the opportunity for a sale. Consequently, I decided that this knowledge is indeed appropriate for anyone who is going to be selling his or her own goods or services.

If you meet with skepticism, start by restating the benefit, then offer proof. What you are doing is showing the customer that you understand what he or she is skeptical of and then backing it up. Now state the benefit once again and expand on it. When you have done this, it is hard for a customer to remain skeptical, assuming that you have a credible source of proof.

For instance, you are selling bumper stickers to college book stores, and you make a statement such as "Mr. Manager, my line of bumper stickers will definitely improve your profits while taking up a minimum of your valuable shelf space" (initial benefit statement). The manager looks at you quizzically and gives a slight shake of the head, indicating doubt. You counter, "Mr. Manager, Carson Bumper Stickers are a proven way of increasing profits with minimal investment in dollars and shelf space" (restating the benefit). "Look, you pay 40 cents per sticker and sell them for $1 for a 150-percent markup, and what's more, they only take up 36 square inches." Still some doubt. "Look at my order book. Texas A & M has given me its fourth order in five weeks!" (offering proof). "If you order now, you'll have delivery in two weeks, and you can make a 150-percent profit like Texas A & M" (expanding on the benefit and offering proof). If the customer still remains skeptical, use closed probes to uncover what is still bothering him, and then use an appropriate proof statement to answer any newly verbalized doubt. The scene goes on until the prospect runs out of reasons to be skeptical or you run out of proof statements. However, it is rare that customers have doubts that they keep throwing out at you. If you have an initial credible proof statement, the sales call should continue on course until you begin the close.

Probably the hardest customer attitude to handle is indifference. You've got a great product, the prospect seems on the surface to be a reasonable person, but when you make your sales call, the prospect just doesn't seem to care. There is only one way to deal with indifference, and that is to use closed probes that may either highlight a dissatisfaction with a product currently being used or disclose other unrealized areas of need that you may be able to support with benefits from your product. You have to think on your feet to come up with appropriate questions in order to keep control of the sales call during a situation like this. You can't merely shoot in the dark in your attempt to uncover dissatisfaction or an unrealized need with your probes; rather, you have to anticipate what problems a person in the prospect's position may face. Knowledge of your product can help a great deal in this situation, because a by-product of becoming more and more familiar with what you are selling is that you understand your customers and their needs more thoroughly. Thus, you are better able to ask the right questions. When you encounter an indifferent customer, you are better able to initiate meaningful probes to uncover areas of need that demonstrate to your prospect that (1) you understand his or her business or concerns and (2) you know your product. Keep in mind that this technique is not a sure-fire way of unlocking an indifferent prospect. However, it does improve your odds and give you a good shot at closing some sales. There is no answer for the prospect who just doesn't show the slightest sign of interest in you or your product. But that's all right. There are plenty of other prospects to call on.

Most people feel that a customer objection is a problem because it usually represents an unwillingness to buy. However, there is one major benefit to an objection, and that is that it shows a prospect's true feelings, allowing you the opportunity to address them rather than just taking blind shots at why the customer appears unwilling to sign the order. The more you know about a customer's feelings, the better off you are.

Sometimes a customer voices an outright objection. Reasons for this may include a misunderstanding, a perceived drawback, or a real drawback. Or your customer may simply not like something about your product. The first two of these objections can be dealt with fairly easily, but the latter two are almost impossible to respond to. In order to know which kind of objection you face, it may be necessary to use some closed probes.

In handling an objection that arises out of misunderstanding, first restate the objection in a question format to uncover any misunderstanding on your part as to what the prospect is objecting to. Then answer the objection directly, so that you clear up the prospect's misunderstanding immediately. Often prospects are skeptical of slick sales talks, so merely saying it isn't so may not be enough. You should be prepared, as discussed earlier, to offer proof. A simulated sales call dealing with an objection arising out of a misunderstanding might go like this:

> **Customer:** No, I don't think I want to carry your line of sweaters in my store this season. They're untested and I don't know if they'll sell.
>
> **Salesperson:** Then what you're saying is that you don't want to carry a line of sweaters that isn't a proven seller?
>
> **Customer:** That's right.
>
> **Salesperson:** I can understand your concerns, and I think you should know that our sweater line is carried in five states and by several merchants in town. I'd be glad to give you several references.

In this scenario the salesperson cornered the prospect by isolating his objection. Once he had isolated the objection, he attacked it and even offered proof. Think of yourself as the customer. Where else can you go? Unless there is a very real drawback, the salesperson using this technique can keep coming back to the prospect time and time again.

When you encounter a perceived drawback, you must first isolate it to be completely sure that you understand the objection. Then you must minimize its effect by introducing new or previously mentioned benefits that are applicable to the objection. This is not a situation that has a perfect answer, since the problem is that the customer *thinks* there is a drawback. Assuming that it is real and not a misunderstanding, your only approach is to minimize the effect it has on the customer's attitude.

The best way to isolate the objection is to repeat it in the form of a question and ask the customer if that is what is really bothering him or her. If the customer tells you that you are indeed correct about the objection, it's time to introduce benefits. When introducing benefits already agreed upon, it will behoove you to seek agreement, such as "We've already agreed that benefit A can help you, haven't we?" If the prospect has previously agreed on that particular benefit, he or she has no choice but to agree with you. The more you can get a prospect to agree with your benefits, the more positive a frame of mind he or she will be in when it comes time for you to go for the close.

When introducing new benefits, make sure that you stress the relevance of the benefit to the *customer's* need. Don't stress benefits that are of no apparent concern to the customer. He or she will merely lose interest, and you will be guilty of a common sin—overselling.

Closing

Now it's time for the final stage of the sales cycle: the close, when you ask for the order. Many people in sales can do everything in the sales cycle except ask for the order, and the result is that they don't get as much business as those who have learned how to go about it.

Knowing *when* to close is one of the first tricks you must master. In all honesty, much of knowing when to close comes from experience, but there are some guidelines to follow.

One time to go for the close is when you feel you've done everything you can to give the prospect reason to buy. You've explained all your benefits, offered proof, possibly even demonstrated the product. If you've done all this, it's time to ask for the order. The worst that can happen is that the prospect says no; you say, "Why not?" and the prospect voices another objection that you hadn't known before. Then you backtrack to that part of the sales cycle.

There are other times, however, when the prospect begins showing signs of wanting to buy. When you see those signs, you know it's time to begin the close.

The close begins with your summarizing all benefits upon which you've previously agreed. This gives the prospect a positive overview of the sales call. You then reach agreement that all those benefits have already been accepted and that the prospect does indeed agree with the stated benefits. Once you have summarized and gotten agreement, you have earned the right to ask for the order. If you get rejected (which is going to happen from time to time) you should ask why. After all, you have also earned the right to an explanation. If, on one hand, the objection is answerable, deal with it accordingly. If, on the other hand, the prospect says yes to your close, you've just gotten the order.

Perhaps the biggest sale any of you will ever close is your first full-time job when you get out of school or college. Make no mistake: It's a sale, and the product is you! After having read this chapter, you should see some approaches to help you in your interviews (sales calls). You should see that using probes can help you uncover exactly what an employer is looking for. Once you know what the employer is looking for, you can sell yourself accordingly. The sell does not have to be a hard sell; it often takes a subtle form, as you casually mention some of your background that matches your employer's requirements and then quietly ask if he or she agrees that your background is helpful, knowing full well he or she has previously said it is. Use your imagination to see what aspects of this chapter can help in an interview situation and use them accordingly. I don't guarantee that this chapter will make you a super salesperson overnight, but I do think that exposure to this material at an early age is invaluable and can lead to the beginnings of some good sales habits that will last a lifetime.

For Further Reading

Mandino, O. G. *The Greatest Salesman in the World.* New York: Frederick Fell, Inc., 1968.

Whiting, Percy H. *Five Great Rules of Selling.* Dale Carnegie & Associates, 1974.

CHAPTER 6

Finance

FINANCE

Finance can be an incredibly complex and technical subject. However, conceptually it can be made fairly easy, because most of it follows basic common sense. Finance as related to student enterprise should be simplified, anyway, but keep in mind that much of what will be discussed here is germane to your personal finances as well. Even if you have a small student business that does not incorporate all of the conceptual topics included here, you should read this chapter carefully, since some of the information may be helpful to you in other aspects of your life. It might help to improve your personal financial structure, which these days can be pretty intimidating, especially if you're looking forward to graduating from college with a $20,000 debt at the age of 20 or 21.

Managing money on the scale of a student business is extremely important, because small business has much less room for error. Moreover, many student businesses are cash-oriented—that is, all transactions are done in cash. Unlike a business that handles its financial transactions through invoices and checks, there is no automatic record of what transactions are taking place.

Finance is managing loans and balancing short-term and long-term debt. Finance is also forecasting your expected level of sales to determine where your break-even point is (for instance, what number of widgets you must sell before you turn a profit). In addition, finance is the understanding of concepts such as risk/return trade-off and the time value of money. Finance deals with managing your bills (accounts payable) as well as the credit you give deserving customers (accounts receivable). These topics are all very important to business owners in their day-to-day operations.

Many a business owner has faced the ironic situation of presiding over a flourishing, growing business that has no money because all the company's cash is being used to finance such things as extending credit to customers as a marketing sales tool, or increasing inventory, or advertising programs to generate sales.

When you become a student business owner, you will probably learn most of these lessons in time; but, unfortunately, the odds are that you'll learn them the hard way. The logic here is simple. Putting it in financial terms, by making a relatively small up-front investment in this book you will improve your risk/return ratio and add profits to your company, giving this chapter a high ROI. (If you don't understand what I've just said, return to this sentence after you've read this chapter and you will.)

Risk versus Return

The concept of risk versus return is as old as capitalism itself. Simply put, the more you have at risk in investment, the higher a return on investment you should demand. The lower the risk, the lower the return. Have you ever heard of someone who made a million dollars without putting forth a lot at risk (lucky gamblers excepted)? In a student business the investment often takes other forms than money. It can be in the form of time, depreciation of resources (such as using your car), or forfeiture of other activities (opportunity cost). One of the more difficult aspects of the risk/return concept is how to evaluate the expected return you should demand. First, there is no clear-cut way in the student business environment to analytically assign a value to the risk associated with a particular venture. There are too many variables; it's a judgment call.

However, you can work backward and figure the rate for a totally risk-free investment. To begin with, the United States government issues debt securities known as Treasury Notes, which are considered risk-free. The likelihood of the United States defaulting on its notes is slim to nil. Therefore, the rate that Treasury Notes (T Bills) command is considered to be the basis for a risk-free investment. There are also money market funds, whose rates are published in the paper, which are considered virtually risk-free. New ventures are considerably riskier than Treasury Notes or money market funds, though, and demand returns in excess of T-Bill rates.

Keep in mind, however, that with a student business neither the investment nor the return is measured in dollars alone. I always felt that the experience gained was well worth the gamble whether I made money or not (although I usually did). However, as the size of the initial investment goes up, naturally so do your expectations. If I had started a venture that required startup capital of $5,000 or more, I would have had a different attitude and sought a financial return of at least the current money market rate. The important thing is to gauge your venture in terms of its risk and compare it to the alternatives so that you don't end up putting a heavy investment in a high-risk/low-return undertaking that will never grow.

(Note: If you are starting a business that requires no money, only time, the risk-free rate would be the amount of money you could earn working in the school cafeteria or other local risk-free jobs.)

Break-even Analysis

This concept is extremely important. Break-even analysis is calculating at what point in sales volume your firm crosses the threshold into profitability. The higher the break-even point, the more units you must sell. Understanding break-even analysis is extremely important to evaluating not only the risk associated with the venture but also the expected returns.

Fixed costs (or overhead) and variable costs, sometimes known as incremental costs, are the two components of determining break-even analysis. Fixed costs are those costs that remain the same regardless of the sales volume. For instance, procuring a business phone for $100 per month would be a fixed cost. The phone costs $100 a month whether you sell one pair of black glow-in-the-dark satin sheets or 100. On the other hand, variable costs are those that rise with each unit of sales volume. For instance, if satin sheets cost $4 each to produce and you pay the salesperson a 20-percent commission on each sheet that sells for $10, the variable costs would be $4 for costs of goods sold (COGS) and $2 for commissions, for a total of $6. In other words, you won't incur a commission cost or a product cost unless you have a sale, so those costs rise and fall with volume. If you've purchased the product already, theoretically you have incurred an inventory cost but not a product cost. However, you can usually arrange terms with your supplier so that you can return whatever you don't sell, and ultimately you don't even incur an inventory cost.

Using the numbers for our satin sheet company, we can do a break-even analysis. The fixed cost is $100 for the business phone. This must be covered by the difference between our selling price and our variable cost. Thus we would calculate:

Sales price		$10
Less:		
Cost of satin sheet	$4	
Commission	2	
Total		6
Contribution		$ 4

Each sheet sold contributes $4 to cover the $100 mountain of fixed telephone costs. If you were to sell only one sheet, you would lose $100, less the $4 contribution from one sale: $96. However, our market research shows that we will definitely sell more than one black glow-in-the-dark satin sheet. Calculating forward, if we sell five sheets, our analysis would be $100 less (5 sheets × $4), equaling a loss of $80. Better, but not there yet. Now if we sell 25, 25 × $4 equals the $100 fixed cost. Presto, the break-even point is 25 black glow-in-the-dark satin sheets. Note: There is a shortcut, which is to divide the fixed cost by the contribution margin ($100 ÷ $4 = 25).

This concept enables you to calculate how uphill the battle will be for you to attain profitability. Obviously, the lower your fixed costs (or overhead), the easier it will be to attain the break-even point. Conversely, the slimmer your contribution margin, the more difficult it will be to reach break-even, as each unit sold makes such a small dent in the mountain of fixed costs. Using this method, you can ask yourself "what if" questions to determine the impact of fluctuations, such as "What if overhead goes up $50?"; "What if sales go down 30 percent?" This is called sensitivity analysis because it allows you to see how sensitive your profits are to variations in costs.

BREAK-EVEN ANALYSIS

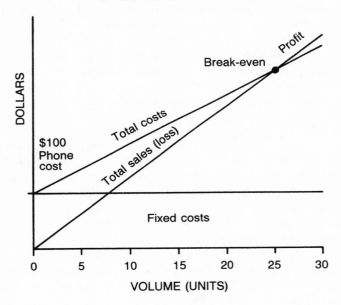

Time Value of Money

Money is a resource that should always be earning a return for you. Even if you leave it in a 5-percent savings account (which is considered risk-free), your money is working for you. Naturally, if you start or acquire a business you will probably invest some of your own money in the venture. You could put your money in stocks or another investment, but if you invest in your own business you do so because you expect that money to earn as much if not more than it would in a savings account, as well as give you an educational experience.

The alternative is to do something along the lines of working as a dishwasher in the cafeteria, where no investment is needed. However, dishwashing is not known for its intellectual stimulation, nor is it a particularly quick way to big bucks. Rather, it's a steady $30- to $40-per-week yawn!

Because of inflation, a dollar today is worth more than a dollar tomorrow. Also, if you have a dollar today you can invest it and immediately begin earning a return. Therefore, if you were offered $100 today or $100 in five years, you would surely take the money today for two reasons. First, you can buy more with the money now than you will be able to in five years. Second, if you were given the $100 today you could invest it in a savings account and earn 5 percent a year for a total five-year compounded interest of $27.71. Think in terms of opportunity cost when you invest in a business, or when you make any investment for that matter. What opportunities are you forfeiting by tying up your money? This is not to say that tying up your money is a bad thing, but just make sure that you keep your eyes open to other opportunities and weigh them carefully against one another.

These three concepts—risk/return, break-even point, and opportunity cost—should enable you to make a better evaluation of your business. They are a framework in which to operate. Don't make the mistake of tunnel visioning and becoming obsessed with whether each and every dollar that you've invested in your business is earning the highest possible return. (Keep it in mind, but don't forget that the experience you are gaining is a return you will not realize until recruiting time. As such it is an intangible that it is difficult to place a numerical value on.)

Working Capital

Working capital is the livelihood of your business. Capital is money and working capital is the amount of money you have to work with. This includes only the money you have that is not tied up and that is easily converted to cash. Perhaps you have wondered how billion-dollar corporations such as Chrysler or International Harvester can get so close to bankruptcy with billions of dollars' worth of land, factories, and other holdings. A very simplistic answer is that they are short of working capital. They have trouble meeting their day-to-day payments. Sure, they have billions of dollars in assets, but they can't turn those assets into cash because those assets are things like manufacturing plants or machine presses. This illustrates the importance of having cash on hand to meet your obligations.

Cash flow is a term used to describe the difference between incoming payments and outgoing payments. Whether business is transacted in currency, checks, or money orders, *cash flow* is a term that all business owners must understand.

My experience with the publishing business serves as a good example here. At first, my company was making soccer programs, then hockey programs, then programs for the NCAA championships. Terrific, I thought. What I didn't understand at that time was that advertisers pay after the program has been printed and circulated. Nevertheless, during the sales cycle we had payroll and expenses to meet, and we were starved for cash. Three weeks after publication we would receive a flood of payments and we would be almost drowned with cash. There was never any doubt about our ability to make a profit. The problems stemmed from the timing of the inflows and outflows of cash—a cash flow problem. If I had known better at the time, I would have taken out a loan sooner than I did. This is a vital lesson that businesspeople, big, medium, or small, should learn early.

The management of cash flow is essential to the longevity of your business. If all things in business were perfect, your accounts receivable (money owed to you by customers) would be paid to you just before you paid your own bills. However, all things are not perfect in the business world, and you need to protect yourself from incurring a negative cash flow. This means having a cushion of cash that you either provide yourself or borrow from the family, friends, or even the bank (which will want you to put up your car or some other asset as collateral). If you don't have a cash cushion, you will always find yourself struggling to make payments and unable to withdraw profits as your cash needs absorb your earnings. For example, if a large potential customer wants credit, you should be in a position to offer credit terms in order to get the business. However, the goods or services used will still have to be obtained and therefore paid for. If you had a small amount of cash in your checking account, you might need all of this money to finance your prospective customer. Even worse, you might need more cash than you have. You would now have a cash flow problem. Eventually, you probably would realize your profits, but it might not be until the end of the semester, which can cause difficulty in terms of timeliness. Your accounting books may say you have profits, but they would be in the form of thousands of dollars owed by your customers. Without the cash, you can't pay your suppliers and employees. If you don't pay these people, they will refuse to do business with you, and you will have no product to sell and no workers. You would, for all intents and purposes, have closed down your business.

How do you control cash flow? One way is to manage your accounts receivable; another is to get credit terms yourself from your suppliers; and yet another is to jam down your overhead and inventory so that you're not paying for things you don't immediately need.

The best way to manage accounts receivable is to make sure they don't balloon out of control. Accounts receivable, or credit, are used as a tool to get customers. You're not a bank and never intended to be, so the only reason you lend money to your customers in the form of deferred payments is as a sales tool. Therefore, don't give exorbitant terms such as 45 days when your customer might accept 10 days' credit. Make sure that your customer is creditworthy and can pay the bill. Many business owners get so carried away by the prospect of a large order that they forget to do a credit check and sometimes end up with a bad debt. Also, send out your bills promptly to get the clock ticking so that payments are received promptly. You can't blame your customers for not paying their bills for 40 days if it takes you 30 just to get the invoice out. If customers haven't paid within the stated terms, chase them down. Don't be belligerent about it, though, unless they wait several weeks past the due date. After all, you catch more flies with honey than vinegar. Take these steps and your accounts receivable will be what they were intended, an affordable sales tool.

If your customer refuses to pay the bill after several months, you have several options. One is what I call the pester approach, which worked for me 95 percent of the time. As the term implies, you become such a pain in the neck that the customer eventually pays just to get rid of you. This means telephoning every other day, stopping by the customer's office, and otherwise being obnoxious. Although this method seems simplistic, it does work. Naturally, a determining factor in whether this time-consuming approach is worth the effort is how much money is at stake.

If the customer in question is a student, an alternative is to approach the dean at school and solicit some advice or help in rectifying the problem. If the customer is not a student, make inquiries to the town's Chamber of Commerce and the local Better Business Bureau. It's a good idea to let the customer know that you're making these inquiries and that it may tarnish whatever reputation he or she has left.

As a last resort you can take the customer to small claims court. First, go to the local county or city court and file papers with the clerk. Sometimes there is a filing fee associated with this process. Then the court serves notice on the defendant, and the proceedings take place within 30 days of serving the notice. If the matter cannot be settled during proceedings, the case goes to trial. This can be a time-consuming process, but in many cases merely the threat of legal action is enough to scare the customer into finally making payment.

Another way of controlling your cash flow is to seek credit terms from your supplier. This frees up cash that you can either reinvest in the business or pocket. If the monies that are freed up are put toward advertising or a direct marketing program, the results are considerably more visible because they create new sales.

Perhaps the single most profitable move I made as a student business owner was to persuade the man from whom I bought my bumper stickers to extend credit terms to me. Instantly hundreds of dollars were freed up, I hired two new salesmen, and five months later we had sold over 50,000 bumper stickers to the states of Massachusetts and Rhode Island, local colleges, and anyone else who would buy them. Credit extended by the printer enabled us to afford the two salesmen, who produced the sales that ultimately resulted in increased profits (I had already exhausted all other available cash sources).

In managing your cash flow, keep all unnecessary costs to a minimum. This means eliminating recurring overhead and minimizing any inventory you hold if it is applicable. Obviously, there is a trade-off between extra inventory and the volume discount you receive from buying in bulk. You must ask yourself if you can afford to keep this inventory. Can you afford not to?

You now should have a feel for the nature of working capital and cash flow. These concepts apply to your personal situation, too, as you must match your expenses with personal income. Also, you should have a savings account (cash cushion) for those times when you might have a temporary negative cash flow. Working capital and cash flow are concepts that you will need to be able to control and manage whether you are a businessperson, doctor, lawyer, or artist. The experience of mastering these concepts is another benefit of running a student business.

Debt

To most people *debt* is a bad word, and rightly so. However, in business, debt (sometimes known as *leverage*) is a tool with which to "leverage" your growth. Like any tool, it can be used or abused.

As sophomores, Richard Taylor and I acquired a refrigerator rental business with a grand total of five small 2-by-2-foot refrigerators that we rented out during the semester. However, the demand far surpassed our meager supply. What's more, after making casual inquiries at nearby colleges, we realized that there was a fortune to be made in fridge rentals. Unfortunately, we didn't have enough money to buy 100 refrigerators (which would come to about $9,000). The solution we turned to was debt. Rick found an outfit that rented refrigerators in bulk. The problem was they wanted payment in advance. So we borrowed the money from a fellow student, rented 70 refrigerators, and proceeded to rent them all out in four days. We paid back the debt with interest several weeks later and consequently increased our profits 639 percent, which was the difference between renting out 70 refrigerators and renting out only five. Without taking the debt we would have missed an opportunity (see table).

Debt, therefore, is sometimes a viable way to finance growth. Without the debt we would have been a much smaller and less profitable operation. Of course, because you are looking at the potential of larger profits (increased returns), there is increased risk (remember risk versus return). In our case the risk was that no one would rent our refrigerators. But we had built in a healthy profit margin, and if a poor response had occurred, we would have reduced our price until we sold out. This is the market forces taking effect. We might not, in this scenario, have made any money, but we would not have lost the whole payment. Surely, for example, we could have found someone to rent fridges for $10 per semester, or if not that then $8 per semester and so on.

INCREASED LEVERAGE FROM DEBT

	5 units (owned)		75 units (5 owned, 70 rented)
Revenue:			
Sales ($60 rental fee)		$300	$4,500
Less:			
Cost of rentals ($40 each)		—	$2,800
Depreciation	$100		100
Labor	10		150
Interest expense*		—	46
Total		110	3,096
NET PROFIT		$190	$1,404
NET BENEFIT OF LEVERAGE		—	$1,214†

* $2,800 at 20% annual interest for one month.
† $1,404 − $190 (639%: $1,214 ÷ $190).

At any rate, the risk with debt is that future expectations will not be met, so you may not be able to pay off the loan. You will have to make up the balance out of your pocket. This is not meant to scare you, but it is important to understand both sides of the concept.

You can see that debt is a means to an end. It's a powerful tool that, when used properly, can be extremely beneficial to your pocketbook. However, if exercised with poor judgment, it can bury you. The adage of gambling therefore holds true in the student business environment: "Never borrow more than you can afford to lose."

Short- and Long-Term Debt

This section is especially relevant to those of you who are going to start ultimately large businesses (over $20,000 in sales) that you might eventually plan to run after you graduate. However, I urge the would-be owners of smaller businesses to read this section too. Not only will it broaden your perspective, but it is also quite possible that your tiny little venture might become big someday.

There are essentially two types of debt: long-term and short-term. In the corporate business world, short-term debt is money that is borrowed for a year or less; long-term debt is money borrowed for over a year. In student business the distinction is shortened because the time frames are smaller. Any money borrowed for a semester or less is short-term debt, and anything borrowed for a longer period is long-term debt.

What difference does it make? You generally pay a higher interest rate on the short-term debt. Basically, short-term debt is meant to get you over a temporary hurdle (like what happened with my refrigerator business), whereas long-term debt is money invested in equipment or programs that will be utilized over a longer period of time. For instance, if you were to start a wind surfing rental business, and the wind surfers themselves cost about $1,200, you would probably want to take a two- to three-year loan so that you could spread out your payments to be more in line with the revenues you took in. For example, if your summer rental revenues amounted to $2,000, with corresponding expenses for repairs and storage totaling $500, this would leave you with $1,500 net. If you borrow in the short term, you might have to pay back $1,440 ($1,200 cost of wind surfer + 20 percent interest) in one year, leaving you with a grand total of $60 for your summer's efforts. If, on the other hand, you borrowed over a long term, three years, your payments would be approximately $600 per year, which would net you $900 per season after other expenses. In other words, since you might be running the wind surfer business for several summers, you don't need to pay back the whole loan in one summer. If you did you would have no money left over to pay your expenses (this is called a negative cash flow problem). With a long-term debt approach, while your total interest cost would be more, the actual monthly payment would be less and you would have money to pay your other expenses as well as taste some of the good things in life.

There are trade-offs to both long- and short-term debt, but the important thing to keep in mind is that you should match the length of your loan to the time frame in which you expect to derive revenues from the project.

Pro Forma Statements

Pro forma statements are predictions of what level of business you expect to do in the next month, semester, or year. They are forecasts; but in the business world, for some odd reason I've never been able to figure out, the statements are called pro formas. Pro formas are important because they help you determine what your break-even point and potential profits may be.

It is prudent to take a guess as to the low, medium, and high potential sales volumes to see how sensitive your break-even point is to a drop or increase in sales. This is called sensitivity analysis, and it allows you to see what is at risk. Obviously, if you have a situation in which a 10-percent decrease in sales is going to cause you to lose your shirt, and

SENSITIVITY ANALYSIS—NEWSPAPER SUBSCRIPTION SERVICE*
How Changes in Sales Volume Affect Profit

	Low		Medium		High	
Sales		$3,000		$4,500		$6,000
Less bad debts						
(1%)		30		45		60
Net sales		2,970		4,455		5,940
Less:						
Cost of goods	$2,000		$3,000		$4,000	
Labor (delivery)	350		500		650	
Advertising	150		150		150	
Total		2,500		3,650		4,800
NET PROFIT		$ 470		$ 805		$1,140

* Assumptions:
Low = 200 subscribers; medium = 300 subscribers; high = 400 subscribers.
Sales price to student per semester: $15.
Cost per subscription: $10.

it would take a 30-percent increase in sales to cause an equal amount of increase in profits, you should carefully examine the risk versus return trade-off to see if you are in the right business. If you ever take a statistics class, this is what standard deviation analysis is all about. The accompanying table shows more clearly how this analysis works and how it can help. The business outlined here is a newspaper subscription service in which the owner sells subscriptions for a semester or a year to *The New York Times* or any metropolitan newspaper that utilizes campus reps to sell subscriptions. This has been successfully done on a variety of campuses across the country. The table shows what happens to expenses and profits if volume drops or rises by 15 percent over the expected forecast. From this analysis, you can determine the risk associated with the venture.

The point of obtaining accurate data in your sensitivity analysis is arriving at an accurate medium or best guess forecast, because it is from this forecast that you take your high and low estimates. There are several ways or combinations by which to arrive at this. The first approach is to look at past history. If sales have been growing at 20 percent per semester for one and a half years, and you don't feel the market has been saturated, it might be fair to project another 20-percent sales increase. However, you might want to work at it another way and forecast by customer or customer group. (This is not always possible as in the newspaper subscriptions business when you deal with the public at large, but when it is applicable it is highly recommended.)

Yet a third approach, for those of you with more than one product, is to forecast by product line. Again, this is not applicable to all businesses, but when it is relevant there is a better chance your forecast will be even more in line with reality. For example, if you ran a business that published a campus advertising coupon book, rented refrigerators, and ran a campus dry cleaning service, you would treat each business unit or product line separately in your forecasts and estimate the semester's revenues by business unit. This gives you three separate sales forecasts, which you then consolidate to give you your net expected gross sales. This is a much more accurate method than just taking the combined total for last year and adding on a flat 20-percent growth rate with no idea of which business unit is going to contribute how much.

Usually a combination of these methods is best. For the truly large business owner who has multiple business units on several campuses with several product lines, a more sophisticated approach is to forecast by business unit, by campus, or by major customer and average them according to their proportion of contribution to overall sales. Also, you can make your estimates strictly by campus, then add them to see how they compare to the totals of your estimates on each product line. Since both totals represent your forecast sales, the numbers should be reasonably close. If they're not, you might dig into them and find out where the discrepancy lies.

Conclusion

We have entered a new era in the eighties. Whereas in the sixties and the seventies economies and markets as a whole were expanding, in the eighties this in general is no longer true. Rather, we are entering a period of stagnation, in which prosperity is no longer a certainty. In such an atmosphere, finance and those who understand its role are becoming more and more important, for it is the finance person who must show ways to increase profits year after year despite stagnant sales volume. Those who understand this subject are going to be more often sought after by prospective employers than those who have chosen to ignore its importance.

We all must enter into debt at one time or another, whether it is a house mortgage or a short-term credit card finance charge, and understanding the concept of debt and its ability to act as leverage is very important to all of us. Finally, dealing with day-to-day cash flow and working capital is a fact of life. Not to understand how this element of our lives functions spells personal financial disaster. So whether or not you are going to operate a large student business concern utilizing the more sophisticated financial techniques, it behooves you to learn about the concepts included here. Now go back to that return on investment analogy in the beginning of the chapter and see if it makes more sense.

CHAPTER 7

Accounting

Accounting is the language of business, and accounting statements tell the story of a business and its performance. Unlike its counterpart, marketing, accounting *is* an exact science. Accounting deals in the past and the present. It tells what has happened with the business at any given time. As such, its primary benefits are (1) to allow you to tell the story of your business; (2) to allow you to spot trends that may eventually spell trouble; and (3) to serve several external functions, such as reporting your taxes. These are very important support functions for your business. However, keep in mind that you are not in the accounting business; you are in the XYZ business, and your job is to sell your product or service. Keep track of your accounting, but don't let it begin to control you. If it does, hire an accountant.

In my sophomore year I was running a vending machine and a refrigerator rental business while starting up yet another venture, in addition to doing my schoolwork. I just had no time to do all the necessary accounting. Barely keeping things in order required three to four hours a week. We hired an undergraduate accounting major who did the books and provided weekly statements consolidating the previous week's activity. We paid him $10 per week, which benefited him because he could do the books much more quickly than I could. Obviously, it benefited me because it freed three to four hours a week of my time. However, whether or not I put that freed time into schoolwork is a point some of my professors would readily debate.

Regardless of who actually prepares the accounting statements, you and your partners must be able to read and interpret them. After all, how else can you tell whether the accountant is doing a good job for you or stealing you blind? I don't mean to imply that accountants usually rob you silly, but you should understand that in order to be a competent manager you need to understand the duties and appreciate the quality of those who work for you. If you do not know whether those working for you are performing a satisfactory job, you may unintentionally cause problems for your venture through their mishaps.

External Accounting Needs

There are three external situations that will require you to have accurate records and that necessitate proper accounting: (1) when you require financing from a bank or any other lender, (2) when you pay taxes, and (3) when you put your student business up for sale.

The first external reason for accounting is procuring financing. Those who lend you money want to be sure that they are lending to a viable business that can pay them back, and not to a fly-by-night operation. The better your bookkeeping, the more professional you appear and the more likely you are to get a loan approved. Would you invest $1,000 with a college student who had no accounting records to show that there was, in fact, even a business? What's more, accounting helps show trends that are developing and that should be exploited. In all likelihood, if you attempt to procure financing, it is because you need money to sustain your growth. How can you show any growth trends if you haven't done the proper bookkeeping?

The next external reason for accounting is taxes. To begin with, you need to have precise figures for your sales, costs, overhead, and profit so that you can accurately report them to the IRS. The only way you can do that is to keep accurate records. This becomes doubly important should the ultimate of unfortunate incidents happen—you get audited. When this happens, you must prove every figure that you have put down on the income tax form. This becomes a real bummer when you have no bookkeeping records to back you up. Many a tale has been told about the unpleasantness of this experience.

The last external situation that demands good accounting is when you put your business up for sale. When you no longer want to be involved in the day-to-day affairs of running a business, you want to get back some sort of monetary benefit. In addition, it is wise to sell out of a business when you feel that it has peaked and reached its potential. Finally, you probably will want to sell your business when graduation time approaches. Whatever the reason, it is vitally important that you have accurate records for would-be buyers. You are selling them the idea that your business can be as profitable and educationally rewarding for them as it was for you. But prospective buyers cannot be expected to take you at your word. They will want bookkeeping records, comparative income statements, bank statements, and balance sheets that tell them how your business has performed. If you don't have this material, there is a risk that potential buyers may shy away from your firm. Since student businesses usually sell for a minimum of several hundred dollars, and often thousands, this could be a most costly error. If you are looking to buy an existing business rather than undergoing the chore of starting one from scratch, stay away from any business whose owner cannot account for stated sales and profits.

Two friends, Scott and Eric, bought a dry cleaning and laundry delivery business from two of their fraternity brothers. The price of the business was set by the school student licensing board. Since the board was run by a roommate of the two previous owners, the price of the dry cleaning business was set at several thousand dollars. Actually, the business was lucky if it took in profits of one-tenth that selling price. The business had no accounting procedures to prove its actual worth. Scott and Eric took a bath in the business once they bought it and realized how inflated the price was. In the real corporate business world, businesses are bought and sold for 10, 20, even 30 times earnings. However, in student businesses the time window is much shorter since you have a maximum of a few years and frequently just one or two years to make back your investment. Thus, the guidelines for setting a price for a student business differ somewhat. A business price should be a reflection of past *and* future potential. Thus, the current value of assets less liabilities (often called owner's equity) plus roughly 50 percent of one year's earnings plus a fee for future potential is a good starting point. At any rate, this story illustrates why you should have accurate bookkeeping as a tool to sell your business.

Internal Needs

The first internal need that bookkeeping satisfies is that it keeps a diary of your business, a ship's log, so to speak. This helps not only with the previously mentioned external needs but also can serve as a memento to you years later when you look back at your youthful college accomplishments. Without getting ridiculously sentimental, I think that this is important. It shows the course your business took and some of the highlights in the form of recording your bigger transactions. When you graduate from college and leave your student business behind, there are two things you take with you—experience and memories. Since you put God-knows-what kind of time, money, and effort into the venture, you might as well take all you can with you, and that includes the memories.

A somewhat less esoteric function for bookkeeping is that, since accounting deals with the past, it shows trends and is a key component of financial analysis. The ability to spot a trend is very important to a student business owner. The advantage of being small is that you can react much more quickly to developing trends than a larger organization can. Thus, the ability to spot a trend and react to it is crucial.

Forecasting, taking past data and extrapolating them into the future, is another internal reason for accurate bookkeeping. Without records of past data, you cannot forecast very well. Forecasting has always interested me because it is such an imprecise science, yet it is so important to the planning process. Forecasting for my businesses was done mostly as a hobby, to see how close I could come to the actual results. Bad accounting usually leads to bad forecasting. As they say in the forecasting business, "Garbage in, garbage out." So, with all the aforementioned reasons why bookkeeping is an essential support function of your business, let us examine some of the actual accounting functions.

Support Journals

The *Cash Receipts Journal* is one of the most important bookkeeping journals for the student business owner. This journal is where you record all cash receipts. When you receive a payment from a customer, you enter the date, the name of the customer, and the amount received. It is also helpful to make a small note under the entry reminding you what the money was for.

There are several ways a Cash Receipts Journal can be set up. The first is to set up one page labeled Receipts and enter all receipts chronologically. If you operate a retail operation that deals only in cash, it is too time-consuming to list the name of every single buyer of your $2 widget remover. Rather, a simple entry like the following, which consolidates everything into one entry, will do:

DATE	ITEM	AMOUNT
Oct. 18	Cash (receipts from sales activities)	$180.00

You would also set up a page for the *Cash Disbursements Journal*. If you deal with a select customer group that makes large purchases (more than $20), enter them individually by name. However, a more common method for this type of select customer set is to put each account on a separate page. The benefit of this is that it allows you to see a customer buying pattern at a glance. This simplifies any forecasting by customer that you may wish to do at the close of the semester. The setup can require a second journal book if allocating a whole page to each account fills the receipts book. The accompanying table illustrates both methods.

The Cash Receipts and Disbursements Journals are important. They allow you to keep track of your cash, and they facilitate any trend analysis you may do regarding sales by account or sales by time period. The cash receipts journal records all cash that comes into your business, giving the amount, date received, and source of cash. The cash disbursements journal records all cash outflow in a similar manner—by amount, date, and to whom the money was paid out. Quite obviously, though, these journals require diligence in recording the information. They become worthless if you arbitrarily skip a day here and there because you simply don't feel like sitting down and recording all your cash transactions. If that occurs, or if you get caught up in other business or school activities, scout around for someone who is an accounting major and hire him or her as a bookkeeper. But remember, make sure that you understand the accountant's job as well if not better than the employee does, for the one who controls the cash controls the business. Getting a bookkeeper because you don't understand the process is a copout and a managerial decision you may live to regret.

The *Accounts Receivable Journal* contains records of all accounts to which you have currently extended credit. Again, this can be done in chronological order, but it should be done by account when applicable. Besides keeping track of how much outstanding credit you have extended, it is also necessary because it tells when you extended the credit, so that you know which accounts are overdue and whether you should follow up. Otherwise, you might let it slide and let several hundreds or even thousands of dollars of much-needed cash go unattended. Finally, this journal lets you spot trends and allows you to forecast what customers will need X dollars of credit next semester, which facilitates your financial planning.

The easiest way to set this journal up is to have the date, the name of the customer, the transaction, the amount of credit or payment, and a total running balance. The next table gives a graphic example. This setup allows you to spot very quickly which customers are reaching the upper level of their credit limit and which customers' bills are overdue.

Also, keep in mind that this is a subsidiary journal to your Cash Journal and therefore must be in sync. Every payment from a credit customer must be entered into the Accounts Receivable Journal to bring down the balance and must also be entered in the Cash Journal to record the receipt of cash. If the journals do not match, you have made a mistake, and one of your customers got a freebie because of your oversight, a mistake few small business owners can afford.

Assuming, through your unending resourcefulness, that you have been able to obtain credit terms from your suppliers, an *Accounts Payable Journal* is necessary. This journal tells

THE MONTANT SHIRT COMPANY
Entries for Cash Receipts Journal*

BY TRANSACTION

DATE	TRANSACTION	AMOUNT
Sept. 20	Cash from Ronny Jaques for 7 T-shirts	$ 35.00
Sept. 21	Cash (receipts for day's sales)	$ 55.00
Sept. 22	Check from college book store for 30 shirts	$110.00

BY ACCOUNT†

College Book Store Account

DATE	TRANSACTION	AMOUNT
Sept. 22	Check for 30 shirts	$110.00
Nov. 15	Check for 2nd order of 30 shirts	$146.40
Mar. 2	Check for 3rd order, 15 shirts	$ 60.00

* This same format is used for the Cash Disbursements Journal.
† Price per shirt varies due to quantity discounts.

you what payments you have outstanding. When this journal is balanced with the Accounts Receivable Journal and combined with the Cash Journal, you should know what your total working capital position is. Consequently, it is the final

THE JUDSON JOHNSON SAILING EQUIPMENT COMPANY
Accounts Receivable Journal

BY ACCOUNT

Babo Sailing Club Account

DATE	TRANSACTION	AMOUNT	BALANCE
Sept. 14	A/R 5 sets foul weather gear	$450	$450
Sept. 26	Payment	200	250
Oct. 14	A/R 1 set foul weather gear	90	340

ACCOUNTING

part of the troika that determines the overall liquidity of your firm.

Generally speaking, the number of creditors you have will be rather small. As with Accounts Receivable Journal, have a separate page for each supplier and enter the corresponding date, creditor, transaction, amount, and balance owed. The following table shows what it looks like. The Accounts Payable Journal should also correlate with the Cash Disbursements Journal. When you make a payment to a supplier, enter it into the Payables Journal and also record a cash disbursement in the Cash Disbursements Journal.

THE SOM COMPUTER DATING SERVICE
Accounts Payable Journal

College Computer Center

DATE	ACCOUNT/TRANSACTION	AMOUNT	BALANCE
Mar. 3	A/P College Computer Center (3 hrs. computer time)	$85.00	$ 85.00
Mar. 10	A/P College Computer Center (1.5 hrs. computer time)	$42.50	$127.50
Mar. 30	Payment College Computer Center	$85.00	$ 42.50

The *Payroll Journal* is applicable to those businesses that will employ fellow students or others. Since most student businesses pay employees by the hour or on straight commission, it is necessary to keep track of their wages and payroll taxes (when applicable) and to monitor whether these employees are productive investments of your money. That is to say, if you are paying someone $4 per hour to sell T-shirts at a booth in the cafeteria, you want to match the payroll expense with the incremental dollars brought in to see whether your profits are enhanced by this activity.

There are several ways to set up this journal, but two ways that I used that worked for us and were not too complicated were as follows. The first is to record the names of all employees chronologically in order of service performed. This includes date, name of employee, number of hours worked or units sold, amount owed, and balance. The other method is to break down the entries into two groups: hourly employees and commissioned employees.

Again, as in the previous journals, when you issue a paycheck you should make a corresponding entry in your Cash Disbursements Journal. This keeps your books in balance. It's a good idea to pay employees weekly, since usually they are students who need their money, too. If they can't get it in a timely manner, they will just go somewhere else where they can. The last thing you need is unreliable labor.

These, then, are the basic support journals you need to run your business. They must all talk to one another—that is, all entries applicable to another journal must match or you will be setting yourself up for unnecessary confusion.

The General Ledger

The general ledger is often considered to be the primary journal of the firm. It is a summary of all activities. So no matter what supporting journal you may need to make an entry in, you should also always make the appropriate summary entry into the general ledger at the end of the semester. For instance, when you record cash receipts in the Cash Receipts Journal over the course of the semester, you should also record the total cash receipts in the general ledger at the end of the semester when you close out your books. Since the general ledger is a summary of all business transactions, it can demand a lot of time. Too much time spent on the general ledger is wasted, though, because that time could otherwise be spent on getting new sales, the livelihood of the business. Thus, if the time spent preparing the ledger gets *too* burdensome, consolidate entries or hire a part-time bookkeeper. Consolidating entries means that instead of entering all purchases separately you enter them as one entry—"business supplies," for example—and let the Accounts Payable Journal record them by individual account.

Two financial statements, the income statement and balance

THE STEELE-ZIMMER COMPANY
Payroll Journal

COMBINED

DATE	EMPLOYEE	TRANSACTION (hrs./units sold)	RATE	TOTAL	BALANCE
Feb. 14	Doug Sacks	5 hrs.	$4.00	$20.00	$20.00
Feb. 14	Greg Winter	2 hrs.	$4.00	$ 8.00	$ 8.00
Feb. 15	Doug Sacks	3 hrs.	$4.00	$12.00	$32.00
Feb. 15	Ellen Shuman	3 hrs.	$4.00	$12.00	$42.00
Feb. 17	Chris Swanton	12 units sold	$1.00	$12.00	$12.00
Feb. 18	Doug Sacks	Payment		$32.00	0
Feb. 18	Greg Winter	Payment		$ 8.00	0
Feb. 18	Ellen Shuman	Payment		$42.00	0
Feb. 18	Chris Swanton	Payment		$12.00	0

BY COMMISSIONED EMPLOYEES

DATE	EMPLOYEE	TRANSACTION Escort hours sold/payment	RATE	TOTAL	BALANCE
Feb. 17	Chris Swanton	12	$1.00	$12.00	$12.00
Feb. 18	Chris Swanton	Payment		$12.00	0

sheet, are discussed at length later in this chapter. Each of these statements consists of line items, which are called accounts. For example, the balance sheet has accounts such as cash, accounts receivable, accounts payable, long-term debt, and several others. Each account in the balance sheet and income statement should be given a separate page in the general ledger. This makes the preparation of these financial statements much easier, since rather than picking through a chronological sequence of entries to get your cash position, you merely turn to the cash accounts page in the general ledger and get your balance.

The general ledger introduces two new terms that are the trademark of the accounting profession—the debit and the credit. For every transaction you record in the general ledger you must make a debit entry and a credit entry. Don't ask me how these names came to be; to be quite blunt, I was always too busy running my businesses to care. However, this double-entry system is standard accounting procedure, and you should be familiar with it. Even now, though you might not be aware of it, you are exposed to it in your bank statements. If you look at the statement, you will see that deposits are credited to your account and checks are debited.

To begin with, since all transactions are entered twice, as a debit and as a credit, the sum of all debits must equal the sum of all credits. There are four procedures governing the application of these entries, which for purposes of clarity I will present together and then discuss individually. Here are the procedures:

- To increase sales, credit the account.
- To decrease sales, debit the account.

- To increase an expense, debit the account.
- To decrease an expense, credit the account.

- To increase an asset, debit the account.
- To decrease an asset, credit the account.

- To increase a liability or owner's equity, credit the account.

- To decrease a liability or owner's equity, debit the account.

Now let me illustrate the process by presenting a few examples. Let us say that you received $1,000 in cash payments from sales to customers in the fall semester. You would then go to both the cash account and revenue account sections of the general ledger and debit cash (increase to an asset—cash) and you would credit revenue (increase in sales). Thus, the entry would look like this:

		Debit	Credit
Dec. 31	Cash	$100	
	Revenue		$100

Let us assume that you borrowed $100 in the fall on November 3 and paid $30 of it off in the spring semester on February 3. In November you would debit cash (increased asset in the form of cash from the loan), and you would likewise credit note payable (increased liability). Then, when you made the repayment in February, you would debit notes payable (for reducing a liability), and you would credit cash (decreased asset). The entries would then look like this:

		Short-Term Debt	
		Debit	Credit
Nov. 3	Cash	$100	
	Note Payable		$100
Feb. 3	Note Payable	30	
	Cash		30

Now let us use an example that would involve a purchase on credit (not to be confused with debit and credit). For example, if you bought $50 worth of pizza on credit for your pizza delivery business on November 15, you would debit pizza $50 (pizza is considered inventory and thus an increased asset as well as increased expense) and credit accounts payable $50 (an increased liability). Eventually, when you made payment (for this example on January 10), you would debit accounts payable (reduced liability), and you would credit cash (decreased asset or decreased expense). The entries would look like this:

			Accounts Receivable	
			Debit	Credit
Nov. 15	Pizza		$50	
		Accounts Payable		$50
Jan. 10		Accounts Payable	50	
		Cash		50

This concept appears somewhat confusing, but it does make sense. When you begin using this system of debits and credits it will become much easier as you climb the experience curve and become accustomed to double-entry thinking.

The general ledger is the primary journal of the business; accordingly, it is used when you total your results at the end of the semester. Because it is the backbone of your accounting system, you should keep it up diligently and make the corresponding entries into the other support journals when necessary. The support journals are also important to the firm, especially the Cash Journal, for if you cannot figure out where the money is going, you stand a dubious chance of returning a profit.

The Balance Sheet

The balance sheet states the financial position of the firm at a particular point in time. There are three components of the balance sheet—assets, liabilities, and owner's equity (see the table on page 129). The balance sheet reflects the financial health of the firm. Therefore, a firm with many liabilities and very few assets would show this on its balance sheet. Banks almost always wish to see a current balance sheet before extending a loan. If they see an unhealthy imbalance between assets and liabilities, they are unlikely to look favorably on the loan applicant. The balance sheet is also important to investors for the same reason; it gives a financial snapshot of a business. Moreover, it is important to would-be buyers of your firm. Since they are in effect buying your assets and goodwill, they will obviously be very interested in your balance sheet.

All assets must be financed from one of two sources: by creditors or by the owners of the business. From this concept is derived an essential formula of accounting: Assets = Liabilities + Owner's equity. The asset side of the balance sheet must always equal the liability and owner's equity side. This is why it is called the balance sheet; the two sides must balance each other.

The first half of the balance sheet lists all assets. These are grouped into two categories: current assets and fixed assets. Current assets are those assets that are easily and readily converted into cash (the rule of thumb is within one semester), including the actual cash the firm has in its bank account. These include such things as accounts receivable, prepaid expenses, and inventories. These assets are considered "liquid."

Fixed assets, as opposed to current assets, are those assets used in the business and from which the firm derives benefits over a number of years (in your case, semesters). They are generally not easily converted to cash. Many student businesses have few or no fixed assets. Some businesses, like my refrigerator rental business, do have them, in that case, the actual refrigerators that we owned. All assets, in accordance with "generally accepted accounting principles" (GAAP), are recorded at the cost of acquisition on original purchase price.

Fixed assets are "depreciated" over the useful life of the asset. This means that, during the time you own the asset, the value you give it in your books goes down over time.

You don't have to keep getting your assets appraised, however. There are formulas you can use to estimate depreciation. The most common formula for determining the depreciation rate is the cost of the asset less remaining salvage value (if any) divided by the useful life of the asset.

For example, if you bought a vending machine for $1,000 that had a useful life of 10 years and no salvage value, the yearly depreciation rate would be $1,000/10 years or $100 per year.

Depreciation is a non-cash expense. In years 2 through 10 you do not pay out any cash for the machine, yet you still incur a depreciation expense. This is useful because it in effect shelters future profits from taxes by lowering your stated net income.

You can now "expense"—treat as a cash deduction in the year you spend the money—certain fixed-asset business purchases up to several thousand dollars. This may have an advantage over depreciating if your business will last just a couple of years. What you *can't* do is to take a cash deduction *and* depreciation for the same item!

The other half of the balance sheet lists liabilities and owner's equity. Liabilities are debts and, like assets, are split into two parts—current liabilities and long-term liabilities. Current liabilities are those debits that have a short time span in which they are to be paid, usually out of current assets. Examples of current liabilities are payroll, accounts payable, and taxes. For a student business, current liabilities rarely extend over 60 days. Long-term liabilities or debt are really self-explanatory. The cutoff point that differentiates between long- and short-term liabilities is usually a year for corporations and a semester for most small student businesses. In the case of a student business, long-term liabilities are any debts that are paid off over a semester or longer.

Owner's equity, the final piece of the balance sheet, represents the investment that the partners or owners of the business have put into the firm. This includes not only the actual cash invested but also those profits that have not been withdrawn, otherwise known as retained earnings. Obviously, the greater the owner's equity, the larger the value of the business.

THE DONAHUE USED CAR CORPORATION
Balance Sheet
December 31, 1983

ASSETS

Current assets:		
Cash	$1,200	
Accounts receivable	6,000	
90-day bank note	1,000	
Inventory (at cost)	4,000	
TOTAL		$12,200
Fixed assets:		
Equipment (tools, etc.)	$1,000	
Less accum. depreciation	200	
TOTAL	800	
NET FIXED ASSETS		$ 800
TOTAL ASSETS		$13,000

LIABILITIES

Current liabilities:		
Accts. payable	$3,000	
Salaries payable	500	
TOTAL		$3,500
Long-term debt:		
10% loan (Dad) due 1984	$2,000	
16% loan (bank) due 1983	4,000	
TOTAL		$6,000
Owner's equity:		
Initial investment	$3,000	
Retained earnings	500	
TOTAL		$3,500
TOTAL LIABILITIES AND OWNER'S EQUITY		$13,000

A large amount of owner's equity shows either that you have invested a large amount of money as owners or that you have left a large amount of profits in the firm.

The Income Statement

The income statement, often called the profit-and-loss (P&L) statement, gives a summary of operations over a period of time. For a student business, do them monthly and then consolidate the monthly P&L statements into semester and school-year income statements. This allows you to know exactly how you are doing at any given time. The semester and school-year statements generally go into more detail than the monthly statement, the purpose of which is to give you a general feel for your profitability. Monthly statements are relevant only to those businesses that do a steady volume of business, as opposed to seasonal businesses that are one-shot deals such as refrigerator rentals, newspaper subscriptions, roommate matching services, and the like. Since all businesses exist, to some degree, to make money, the income statement is an important document. It reflects whether you are attaining your goal of making those dollars that you envisioned when you undertook the venture.

The best way for a student business owner to set up an income statement is to divide it into these parts. First comes revenues or sales, less discounts and returned merchandise. This gives you *net* sales. Second, the variable costs, or the cost of goods sold (COGS), are subtracted from this number to give what is known as the gross margin. It is important to watch the gross margin; it may slowly shrink as suppliers inch their prices up or you give liberal discounts to lure large customers to your firm. Now that you have calculated the gross margin, you list the overhead, which is often known as fixed costs. Once the overhead section is totaled, it is then subtracted from the gross margin and presto, you have the gross profit. Taxes are then subtracted when applicable, and this results in the goal of your travails, the net profit. It is not very difficult to prepare an income statement, provided

THE BLAKNEY BUMPER STICKER COMPANY
Income Statement
December 31, 1983

Revenues:		
Sales	$25,600	
Less discounts	1,200	
NET SALES		$24,400
Costs:		
Cost of goods sold	17,000	
GROSS MARGIN		$ 7,400
Less fixed costs:		
Commissions	$ 2,560	
Telephone	200	
Salaries	1,500	
Supplies	200	
Miscellaneous	300	
Total		$ 4,760
GROSS PROFIT		$ 2,640
Less taxes	$ 320	
NET PROFIT		$ 2,320

that you have been diligent in keeping up with the support journals.

Federal Taxes

It scared the hell out of me in my freshman year when I first realized that along with the fun of presiding over my own business I also had to deal with the issue of taxes. However, it is not quite so bad unless you happen to net a good chunk of money in one year, and even then there are some ways of reducing your taxable income.

I am not going to drone on about various tax approaches, forms, methods, and so on, since the Internal Revenue Service (IRS) has prepared booklets that do a much better job than I could. These are listed at the end of the chapter. However, here are some basics.

First, let me address federal taxes that apply to us all. To begin with, unless you earned over $3,300 in one year (January 1 to December 31), you do not pay any federal income taxes. Unless you have incorporated, which only very large student businesses do, your net profit is figured as personal income. If you made over $3,300 and own your firm by yourself, you simply file Schedule C, "Profit or (Loss) from a Business or Profession," along with the normally filed 1040 IRS form. If you have elected to go into a partnership, file Form 1065, "U.S. Partnership Return of Income."

Deductions

Even if you find that your reported income will exceed $3,300, there are still some avenues for you to investigate that can lower this number, provided a major proportion of your yearly earnings come from your business. First, if you have any assets that are utilized for your business, such as your car or other equipment, you can depreciate them and deduct the amount from your business income. The simplest and most commonly used form of calculating depreciation is called straight-line depreciation, by which you calculate or otherwise determine the useful life of the asset in question. You then divide the cost of the asset by this figure. For example, if you purchased a $200 calculator for your business that had a useful life of five years, straight-line depreciation dictates that the yearly deductible depreciation would be $40 ($200 ÷ 5). In the case of your car, which is not used entirely for business, you may find it simpler to deduct a standard mileage rate, which in 1982 was 20 cents per mile. Additionally, other expenses pertaining to the operation of your business are allowed. For example, if you are a business or economics major, you may pay for most of your books and educational expenses out of your business. For an exact description of how this particular deduction works, write the IRS for "Treasury Regulation 1, 162–5." This aspect alone may make running a student business worth the time regardless of the cash you make from the venture.

132

Other Taxes and Related Matters

There are other state, local, and payroll taxes, which I will briefly describe here. If you are going to be hiring employees, the government requests that you file Form SS-4 "Application for Employer Identification number." If you do file this form, the IRS will mail you quarterly and year-end payroll tax returns, which you complete and send back with a check for the taxes you have withheld from employees. Before an employee works for you, he or she should fill out a federal W-4 form. If you perceive this as a hassle, you may request your employees to begin individual labor businesses such as "Mike's Labor Services." This approach means that Mike is simply a business you are contracting with, and thus it is his problem whether he pays his taxes on time or at all. However, if you do follow this practice, you must file a federal Form 1099, "Statement of Miscellaneous Earnings," plus Form 1096, "Annual Summary and Transmittal of U.S. Information Returns." If all this sounds like a real drag, you now know what the deregulation debate is all about.

In any state that has a state sales tax, all sellers of retail goods to consumers are required to collect sales taxes. The means by which you do this is a resale permit or state seller's permit. This permit allows you to buy goods from wholesalers without paying sales tax yourself. You will usually receive a monthly or quarterly form from the state (a.k.a. the payroll tax forms), which you fill out and send back with the sales taxes you have collected. In a roundabout way, the government has made you its tax collector.

The last subject related to taxes and such is local selling permits. These permits register you in the town(s) where you are doing business and can usually be found in the town clerk's office at the town hall. Some towns do not require them, but most do. In the town where I registered, the registration process took about 15 minutes.

This discussion has been a very brief overview of the subject of taxes, which of course fills entire textbooks. I feel that, for a student business doing sales of less than $10,000 per partner, the related headaches are not going to be much to worry about. If you intend to run a large business with the necessary related tax-reporting efforts, use this section as a primer or guideline and get the IRS documents listed at the end of this chapter. Also keep in mind that tax regulations and guidelines are notorious for multiple revisions and changes, so be sure you have the latest information.

Many people take four to six years to learn about accounting and taxes in depth. However, for the average student business owner the information within these pages should suffice. If you feel that the size of your business necessitates a deeper level of discussion, there are additional sources of information. It is important for you to be exposed to these subjects, for you will surely face them in the future, and if you ignore these time-consuming but important facets of small enterprise, you are certainly doing yourself a disfavor.

For Further Reading

The following IRS publications are available free at your nearest IRS office:

Publication 17, "Your Federal Income Tax," tells how the federal income tax system works.

Publication 334, "Tax Guide for Small Business," a must for any medium to big student business.

Publication 535, "Tax Information—Business Equipment and Operating Losses," tells how to deal with depreciation and the deduction of operating losses.

Publication 539, "Withholding Taxes and Reporting Requirements," explains how payroll withholding taxes work and gives the withholding tables to calculate tax.

Publication 541, "Tax Information on Partnership Income and Losses," describes how to evaluate taxes on a partnership.

Publication 1066, "Small Business Tax Workbook."

Also recommended:

Benjamin, James; Arthur Franca; and Robert Strawser. *Financial Accounting*. Dallas: Business Publications, Inc., 1975.

CHAPTER 8

Keys to Success

In the world of small business, and especially to the first-time student entrepreneur, every scrap of useful information is helpful. My years in college led me through several undertakings, all in different areas—service businesses, wholesaling, retailing, and vending, to mention a few. Some worked out very well; some didn't. As a matter of fact, a few were horrendous testaments to my ignorance. But along the way I learned a few basic dos and don'ts that, had they been known beforehand, would have saved me considerable pain and suffering. Following are some ways to avoid common pitfalls and improve your chances of success. Some of the information applies to one type of venture more than others, but it should help you develop a business instinct.

Know What You Want to Get Out of Your Business

Setting your objectives is really a reflection of what you want to get out of your business. Essentially there are two very distinct attitudes that have a lot to do with this decision. Are you in it for the money or the experience? Perhaps both. Some students own their business out of sheer necessity. They must either put themselves through school or pay for that new $10,000 Scirocco that they just put a down payment on. Whatever the reason, these kids are in it for the bucks pure and simple. On the other side of the coin are students who start a business, then sink all of their profits into financing its expansion. They just want to see their sales grow for the experience of being able to roll out their own marketing plan from top to bottom. It doesn't hurt the ego, either, to be the proud owner of a business that grosses $20,000 in sales per year. That's an accomplishment, whether it's a moneymaker or just marginally profitable! The thinking among this set is that profits will come in due time as overhead levels off. The important part is to get those sales up, up, up.

These two approaches need not be mutually exclusive. In fact, a mixture of the two is ideal because it motivates from two directions. In the first place, there is nothing wrong with becoming somewhat profit-oriented. Welcome to twentieth-century capitalistic America! If you also have an educational interest this leads to an intellectual approach—looking for problems and solving them, experimenting with new products—and the option to take a risk. If you take the risk, you may lose a little, but you may also make a few bucks. The combination of capitalistic spirit and intellectual curiosity makes for a well-rounded attitude about going into business for yourself while in school. It provides the two essential ingredients for a successful entrepreneur: the drive for profits and the guts to take a chance on an idea that you hope will pay off in the long run. It is this creative ingenuity that has made America what it is today. Unfortunately, government has made startups a bleak prospect for the small business. But you're in school, where market forces aren't totally in effect, so you don't have to worry so much about that.

Mike Swanson, for example, a sophomore engineering student at Duke University, started a business designing and printing T-shirts and the like. One of his projects is a painter's hat Mike designed and bought from a wholesaler that said, "Go Duke—Go to Hell Carolina." Mike took the risk and ordered 1,000 hats, not knowing if he could unload the lot. If they didn't sell, Mike would have been left with 1,000 hats and an invoice for several hundred dollars. At last count he had sold over 800. I would estimate that a profit of $400 to $600 was the eventual result of this venture. His success is a reflection of his combination of a profit motive and the willingness to take a risk. Just imagine, that could have been you!

If you decide that you are in it for the bucks, then in all likelihood a service business is your best prospect, since it usually requires a minimal up-front investment. Most students who want to start a business for purely monetary reasons don't want to make a large investment to get things off the ground. After all, why bother sinking a fistful of bucks into a venture to make your money when you could just as easily make some money working a part-time job at little or no risk? The answer depends on the individual. Some people like the excitement of running their own ship; others feel it's worth it to spend a couple of hundred dollars to get it off the ground. But by and large, the easiest compromise is to start a service business that has an enticing expected return and requires little or no investment.

Duncan Donahue, of Norwell, Massachusetts, is a great example of this. Duncan started an advertising coupon booklet; he sold local retailers an advertising place in his booklet for $100. He distributed 10,000 of them to neighboring colleges in Boston. There was a total investment of approximately $5 to mimeograph rate sheets, and he was off and running. Duncan didn't make millions off this venture, but profits averaged about $50 a week for a whole school year. Considering the investment in both money and time, this was not bad at all.

The whole concept of a service business revolves around providing labor rather than goods. Good business people usually don't pay for labor services until they have been completed, so there is a minimal up-front investment in the product you are providing, namely labor. As soon as you get involved with providing tangible products, you incur all sorts of headaches, such as inventory control, up-front money, and cash shortages. I don't want to discourage you from this type of business, but it is certainly more challenging. If you are starting your first venture, a service business is much simpler and can be just as financially rewarding. On the other hand, a product-oriented business does offer the challenge that someone who wants practical business experience is looking for, as well as often providing a lucrative return. So it all boils down to "What are you in it for?"

Distinctive Competence

To start a business and have it catch hold, you must have a "distinctive competence." Without a distinctive competence there is absolutely no reason for anyone to buy your product or service over anyone else's. You must be cheaper, or more convenient, or so new that you have no competition. In the case of a company like McDonald's, its distinctive competence is the fact that the stores are so standardized that the one in Hawaii is exactly the same as the one in Bangor, Maine. There are plenty of hamburger places, but you know that at McDonald's the burger always has the same great taste and it doesn't cost an arm and a leg. You might find a better burger, but why waste your time when there's a McDonald's right around the corner and you know exactly what you're going to get? You must choose or invent a distinctive competence, develop it, and use it as much to your advantage as possible. This includes advertising and promoting it to the public so that people may derive the benefits of your distinctive competence. You may want to improve it more, in which case you may very well need to sink some bucks into further development. Your objectives are directly influenced by your distinctive competence, so you should decide what your distinctive competence will be and plan around it.

Think Big

When you start a business, think BIG! Some people may not share my view, but I say if you're going to do it, go all the way. If your business does well on your campus, why wouldn't it work on five other campuses? No reason at all, if you have the right attitude. If you think big from the very beginning, you will formulate your objectives accordingly to facilitate the transformation from an embryo to a little giant. If you have a campus-oriented business, look upon your own campus as a test market for expansion to other campuses. This means you have to look at your own campus business as a warm-up or as a way of ironing out the kinks of a much bigger, more involved program. With a business that concentrates most of its efforts off the campus, you may wish to set target sales goals at the end of every two weeks or a month. This can also be applied to an on-campus enterprise. Be realistic with yourself, and don't set ridiculously high projections. A young woman had a small but flourishing catering business, which she stopped running because she was not reaching her projected sales quotas. But when you set 130-percent growth targets every month, what can you expect?

Walk Before You Run

Right after having told you to think big, I'll now warn you of the danger of rushing when you start up. This on the surface would seem to contradict the belief in thinking big; you can't get big by taking your time. The problem comes when you find yourself growing so fast that you just don't have enough time to do all the little things that need to be done. When those little things aren't done for a period of time, the credibility of your firm will begin to crumble.

For example, Todd dropped out of college to start a vending machine operation on several college campuses. The vending machine business is lucrative, to put it mildly. Todd expanded so fast that his machines started running out of products at an above-normal rate because he was not properly staffed. As soon as people couldn't take advantage of the distinctive competence of vending (convenience), they began to complain to the college administration. They also resorted to hitting the machines with vacuum cleaners and other assorted objects. Eventually Todd's vending operation collapsed because he was asked to leave several campuses and because he experienced abnormally high damages to his machines. The lack of credibility ruined his business. People didn't respect his operation.

The implication of the above example is that it is imperative to make sure that you weather the growth process smoothly. You can do this in one of two ways or in a combination of the two ways. The first way for those of you who can scrounge up the bucks is to add employees who aren't immediately productive, knowing that in a short time enough sales will have been added to keep their little fingers busy. In other words, it's better to be overstaffed than understaffed. That way your credibility will remain intact because you will be prepared for emergencies. If your credibility lapses and people can't depend on your service or your product, they won't bother coming back. Consumers are notorious for looking out for themselves and having little or no loyalty, which is perfectly natural, so it's up to you to make your growth process a smooth one. Financing extra employees in readiness for increased sales is a viable way to accomplish this.

A second method is to plot out each week carefully and see what the increased sales will add to the work schedule. When you see what you need done, you can adjust accordingly. This calls for a constant review process, and it probably won't be too long before it just becomes too time-consuming. It would seem more sensible to borrow money and spend the freed-up time gathering new accounts or increasing the ones you already have.

When your company is turning a profit, if you leave the money in the firm, it can be put toward new employees or added inventory to ensure against running out of stock. This is called internal financing because the company is financing itself. For the vast majority of you, this will in all likelihood be how you finance the growth of your business. Since ordinary growth requires capital to pay for such things as added employees, inventory, and accounts receivable, fast growth puts an added strain on your resources. Be aware that you could start growing so fast that you go bankrupt financing your growth. You have to develop a sense of how much you can manage in terms of both time and money.

Be Flexible

Now let's assume that you have your objectives set and your fledgling enterprise is off and running. Great! I told you it could be done. After a short while you should review your objectives. In the infancy of your business, many things change, and you may want to rewrite your objectives after a short trial period.

Jack Veasy and his partner are a strong case in point, although both had already graduated from the Harvard Business School when they started their cocktail lounge/restaurant, The

Hampshire House, in Boston. They prove that a change in objectives can turn mediocrity into success. Originally the concept had been to provide a businessman's club with a rustic library decor. Reviewing their objectives after six months, they decided to try to attract a younger crowd. The present situation was yielding unacceptable losses, and the change to a younger clientele demonstrated a desire to change the original objectives. The result: they added a singles' bar downstairs that catered to a heavier-drinking crowd. Mr. Veasy and his partner are now the proud owners of a profitable, successful dining and drinking establishment that caters to a much younger group of people than they originally planned. (Note: The establishment is so successful now that one television network based the series "Cheers" on it.)

You may find yourself in a similar situation—your basic idea was right but the concept is a little off—and adjust accordingly. That doesn't mean you should change things for the sake of change, but rather adjust to a situation you hadn't previously planned for. Don't review your objectives *too* early, however. You have to give your business a chance to get off the ground. Success doesn't happen overnight—at least not all the time.

Partnerships

Getting the right partner can be one of the keys to getting an idea off the ground. I am a big believer in partnerships at this age. Having a partner can really help you move an idea into place because there's someone else to answer to. Assuming that you haven't picked a real turkey, you will find that having a partner puts low-key pressure on you to start doing your part of the startup work. After all, the two of you have probably discussed the idea at length, so were you to just sit on your duff and let the idea pass you would look like more of a talker than a doer. I found that when I had partners we would delegate tasks to each other. If one of us did nothing, the other would give that person a severe tongue-lashing, and usually that was incentive enough for me. When you try to launch an idea by yourself and then put it on the shelf, you have no one to get on your back to get you going. A partner motivates you when you start thinking about packing it in.

If you should take on a partner who has also read this book, you may have a battle for majority control. I strongly recommend that you gain majority control when possible. Majority control affords you the convenience of more input into decisions, since you in fact are the majority owner. More important, it exposes you to the maximum number of decisions, thus giving you increased business experience. If you are in it for the money, naturally this also means you take home a correspondingly larger share of the profits, although each partnership arrangement is different and you may elect to split 50–50 for one reason or another. Whatever your drive, money or experience, majority control gets you more.

Now don't misunderstand me, that doesn't imply that I advocate getting it at all costs. If you have a very stable partner relationship, don't rock the boat. One of the most successful businesses that I was involved in was with a partner who split everything with me 50–50. However, if you have the idea and really take the leading role, control is a reasonable reward for your efforts. The assumption is that you are the idea getter *and* the drive behind the operation. That's not to say your partner is a slouch, either. If you are starting what looks to be a very small venture the objective of which is to provide a couple of extra bucks for weekends, a squabble over what is really very little obviously is not worthwhile. However, if your small venture ultimately has large aspirations, the time spent early on defining who does what and gets how much is well worth it.

If you have a majority position in your company, it is logical that you have to give up something in return for this privilege. This takes the form of either a larger monetary investment on your part or a larger share of business duties, which usually means increased responsibility for those things that go right as well as those things that go wrong. There is really no right or wrong way to set up your partnership in terms of what you give up for what you get. Obviously, you are unlikely to find a situation in which you put up no capital, have minimal job responsibilities, and still retain a healthy share of equity. In theory, the person on whom the business is most reliant is the person who brings in the lion's share of new accounts, since that is the life blood of any venture. You've got to get those early sales to get the gears whirling, and if that super salesperson leaves, the business slows to a grinding crawl unless there is someone readily available to fill the gap. Any new venture that has good salespeople begging to join is in an enviable (and unusual) position. Regardless of how you decide who gets what, there is an allocation of responsibilities.

It is absolutely essential to your future relationship with your partner that these responsibilities be clearly defined so that each of you knows what he or she is expected to do. Put it down on paper so that there is no chance of misunderstanding two or three months later. Probably the number-one reason for dissolved partnerships is lack of communication, especially in the area of defining responsibilities.

Communication

When your partner leaves something undone that later snaps back in *your* face, the immediate temptation is to punch the first object that makes the mistake of crossing your path. Since the problem usually stems from a lack of understanding as to what the partner was expected to do, a written definition of everyone's responsibilities is an easy solution. The root of the problem is communication. If you and your partner communicate at all times, snafus will be minimized, and so will growing pains. The most important part of communicating is defining responsibilities.

But there are other areas of communication that should not be left unattended. Whose car will be used, compensation, future capital needs, and which partner is going to supply them are all questions that should be discussed *before* they arise. Aside from this, there are times when you and your partner will need each other's help. Communicate those needs as early as you possibly can. Having someone dump a couple of hours of work in your lap that must get done at the last minute can play absolute havoc with your blood pressure.

One of the more common methods of preventing a communication breakdown is a weekly meeting between partners. At the end of the meeting you should draw up a list of unresolved issues. That gives you a general idea of the agenda to be discussed the following week.

Communicating is a skill, and if you can learn to master it before you leave college you will certainly have a feather in your cap. A manager in any business is only as good as his or her ability to get the work done. The key to getting work done by employees or other managers is communicating needs and wishes to them effectively. The same holds true for you as a student business owner, except in this case the person on whom you must concentrate your communication efforts is your partner. One key to the art of effective communication is not taking anything for granted. Never assume that your partner knows about anything that you aren't absolutely sure he or she knows. That way you leave a minimal margin for error in communicating, and you are one step closer to being an efficient management team.

Because in most student-run businesses there are many times when you and your partners must fill each other's shoes, another key to a well-managed enterprise is flexibility. Consequently, after a month or so, switch responsibilities with your partner for a week or two, in order to get an idea of what is called for in his or her role in the business. Aside from providing a better understanding of your partner's situation, it allows you to get some training in that area. If you should be called upon to fill in for any reason, you will already be familiar with what needs to be done.

Several years ago two ambitious guys, Bob and Neil, landed the concession for the Babson College snack bar. Babson had a practice of allowing students to buy the concession rights. Each application was judged by a student licensing committee, which selected the most promising applicant. The price, $2,500, was paid to the seller, who was not allowed to run the concession more than one year. This practice has been stopped because the student managers, realizing that there was a golden chance to *clear* $15,000 to $20,000 in a year, began to set records for new lows in academic achievement. Finally, the college was forced to turn the management over to a professional catering service.

Previous to the snack bar's demise as a student-run operation, Bob and Neil put together the winning proposal and won rights to the concession. They probably ran one of the tightest, best-managed operations in town (as well as pulling down respectable grades). How? Easy. They communicated on a regular basis. Each knew what the other was doing, and, more important, each knew what he himself had to do. Aside from a strong communications effort, they also at one point exchanged duties for two weeks so that in case one were indisposed the other could always cover for him. There was a minimal allowance for human error, as each problem had a solution and some even had backup solutions. Their business, I would estimate, grossed close to $100,000 a year. Believe me, when you've got that kind of cash going in and out, as well as 2,000 students to serve, you had better be a damned good manager or you could be out of some very serious bucks. If you anticipate problems and communicate effectively, you've got half the battle won.

Motivating Employees

One of the biggest problems encountered in my four years of college business was that of motivating employees, who were also college students. There are several aspects to this problem. The first is that it is difficult to form a boss-worker relationship with people who are your peers in all other aspects of college life. You really can't take a tough-guy approach; but, on the other hand, if you are too easygoing your employees can easily mistake your attitude for not caring. If that happens, their reliability becomes questionable because if you don't care, neither will they. So, the best course of action is a middle-of-the-road approach, which requires you to be stern when called for and an easygoing boss the rest of the time.

A second aspect of motivating employees is a monetary one. How much do you pay the people who work for you? Keep in mind that the cheaper the labor, the lower your prices can go, which gives you a competitive advantage in the marketplace. On the other hand, you want to make sure that your workers show up when you want them to and that they do a good job when they are working. If you are employing them as salespeople, a commission or commission plus base salary are two options available.

A case in point of properly motivating employees economically was a friend, Eric Rahn, who bought an existing dry cleaning service that provided door-to-door pickup and delivery for students who didn't have a car. In addition, customers were billed monthly rather than having to pay cash. The prices were slightly higher than those at the shop in town, but apparently it was worth it to most students. Eric's main problem was to get reliable employees who would pick up and deliver two nights a week. Because his employees were students too, they also were subject to midterms and papers and everything else that makes up academic happiness. Eric's answer was to have rotating schedules so that if someone was unable to work he had a reserve. Additionally, he paid a dollar over minimum wage. (A commission rate was impractical because it was doubtful that it would have yielded much of an increase in sales to justify the expense.) The result was that Eric had a dependable work force that individually took home $20 per week for four hours of work. His method was expensive and lowered profits, but it saved Eric plenty of headaches. There is definitely a trade-off between higher profits and increased headaches. Essentially you have to pay for dependability, and that's exactly what Eric did.

Weekly Financial Analysis

One of the best policies I ever implemented, which not only gave me accounting practice but also helped considerably in my perception of our growth process, was the use of a profit-and-loss statement for the previous week of sales (see Chapter 7). This gives you an idea of what profits are for the week. It also gives you something to compare the following week's sales and expenses with. As you compare, you can check to make sure that no single expense is rising at a higher rate than your sales. The time spent on drawing up a P&L statement should be no more than 30 minutes if you have proper bookkeeping procedures. When your cash reserves can't meet your current expenses, you've got a problem. What can make this even more frustrating is having money owed to you that is not due for a week or two. Theoretically you have the dough, but in reality it is not in your hands, which doesn't help you with your creditors at all. Your P&L statements should be a tool to safeguard against this event. But remember, it is just a tool, nothing more, and it is only as good as the person who prepares it!

File for a Tax Number

You've undoubtedly heard the cries from the business community about how government regulation stifles business growth by requiring so much manpower to fill out the necessary forms. The lion's share of this regulation concerns taxes. I hate to be the one who brings bad news, but as painful as it is to say, if you start your own business you have to file tax returns. Although you should file, you will probably not have to pay. File your taxes if you have a business with over $5,000 in sales. In all probability you won't owe a dime, since you are allowed by law to earn up to $3,300 tax-free as a student. Additionally, you could protect a lot of your leftover cash (profit) by deducting on Schedule C for things like mileage (remember, every mile is a 20-cent deduction), phone expenses, entertainment expenses, and general overhead. Unless you have an unusually large business, after all these deductions you should have the bulk of your taxable profit sheltered. If you find yourself with a business that is making an enormous taxable profit in spite of itself, consult with a professional accountant; you obviously can now afford one.

The primary reason I recommend filing tax returns even if you don't owe any money is to learn how the tax system works. You will be much more able to cope with your personal tax returns as a result of the experience of filing for your student business. It is important to remember that every area in your business is a learning center—an area where you can gain vast amounts of practical experience—and taxes are no exception. Rise to the occasion and meet the challenge.

Time—Your Biggest Resource

There is one considerable problem with thinking big and that is the time factor. After all, your parents probably sent you to college to get a degree and not to become Howard Hughes, Jr. If you are a grade-oriented person, chances are you will elect to maintain a respectable market share and keep profits pretty steady. However, there can be a happy compromise between growth and academic pursuit. The answer is time budgeting.

Time budgeting is as simple as it sounds. If you can budget your time carefully enough you can have, as Dr. Pangloss said in the French classic *Candide,* "the best of all possible worlds." That means you can have your business, achieve academic success, and still have time left over for the important things in life—like parties. If you carefully analyze your day, you will be amazed at how much waste there is. Think of how much time you waste watching drivel on TV or dawdling after lunch. If you were to trim some of that time you would have about an extra hour and a half a day to divide among business, school, and social pleasures. That works out to anywhere from seven to ten hours a week, a lot more extra time than you ever thought you had. At one point in my junior year I found myself with four businesses, and for survival I learned to recognize and utilize five minutes here and ten minutes there. Otherwise, I would never have done all the odd jobs that needed to be taken care of. There was always an abundance of spare time after dinner, when most people just hung around their rooms playing their stereos before sauntering off to the library. That was when I found the time to do all the necessary accounting work for all of my businesses, thus freeing up several hours of time Sunday afternoon, when I usually studied. Ironically, that busy semester was my most rewarding academically.

Another effective trick for better use of your time is a "things to do" list. By just writing down what must be done in order of priority you facilitate the planning of your day. This is an essential skill for corporate executives, who are often confronted with too much to do and not enough time in which to do it. If you can develop this kind of self-organizing approach, you will have a marketable skill to offer future employers. And that's what at least part of college is about: getting a job and the skills to do that job. Those skills need not be confined to future business executives. Being organized and developing a sense of the importance of budgeting your time efficiently will benefit you in the long run no matter what your profession is.

Ethics

Ethics is a set of standards that acts as a parameter of the decision-making process. Using good ethics is habit-forming. If you run your own business in college, it will probably be your first exposure to the world of business. Consequently, you will for the first time face situations that may require some very difficult decisions. Some people instinctively have strong moral principles, while others have terrible ones. But the majority of us lie somewhere in the middle, and outside factors and pressures may often influence our eventual decision.

Rationalizing is the root of most unethical decisions. It happens over and over. The majority of people don't make an unethical decision with the thought, "Great, I really took that turkey to the cleaners." Rather, most people justify their decision based upon a multitude of rationalizations, the most common of which is "He didn't have to buy from or sell to me if he didn't want to." Be honest with yourself. If you're going to cheat or rip someone off, at least admit to yourself you're being dishonest. Many essentially honest people make dishonest decisions by rationalizing and really do feel that they're still honest people at heart. If they admitted to themselves that what they are doing is dishonest, they would probably think twice before making the decision.

What happens if you are discovered making an unethical decision? Teddy Kennedy has never lived down a little mistake in judgment he made in school, which at the time probably didn't seem like a big deal. Moreover, how much money would you actually derive from being unethical? Compare it to what your expected lifetime earnings will be, and you will probably see that you just sold your moral standards for a pretty cheap price.

Here's a very personal example. (The names are changed in deference to some individuals who were less guilty than others.) My freshman year I lived next to a senior who owned a thriving business. I had a lot of respect for Brian, who took me under his wing and showed me the ropes of college life. Near graduation I asked if I could buy his business. He told me its sales volume and what assets I would inherit, and I finally paid his price. Unfortunately, I took him at his word and got burned. It turned out that a significant percentage of the assets, which were valued at several thousand dollars, weren't his at all. They had been lent to him by his biggest supplier in return for the large volume of business that the supplier was receiving. In other words, Brian had sold me assets that weren't his. When I went to the supplier to set up terms for the next school year, I received quite a shock when he asked for his equipment back. That was one of the most annoying moments of my life, and I vowed to regain both my self-respect and my lost money. I'll never forget the look of astonishment on the face of one of the partners, who thought he had left me behind for good in Boston, as I walked into his London office. I walked out with my money and my self-respect intact.

It is unfortunate that Brian and his partners sold their integrity for a mere $400 each, when they were all probably making $15,000 to $25,000 a year in their new jobs a month after graduation.

From my experience and observation, there are pitfalls that are common to unethical decision making. I offer no solutions, for you will have to deal with these decisions yourself. I cannot tell you what your moral fiber is; I can just warn you of problem areas. One of the most tempting decisions is the selling of your business. The stakes are relatively large, and in most cases the act takes place toward the end of senior year; if the transaction blows up in your face, you will probably be long gone and won't have to live with it. Moreover, the buyer often is new to the game and as such is ripe for being taken advantage of.

Another common pitfall is walking away from a supplier's bill when you've gone home for the summer or after graduation. If you live in another state or a different part of the country, there is little likelihood that the supplier will come after you. Remember, however, the golden rule you memorized as a child. How would you like it if it were done to you? This happened to me once (by a student who advertised with me), and it told me a lot about the person in question.

An additional example is delivering a product or service that is not what you promised or overstating the value of your product or service. There is a fine line between pure sales hype and deliberate misinformation; therefore, this is the hardest area in which to make a clear-cut judgment.

Forming good ethical standards does have more than intrinsic value and doesn't necessarily preclude a financial payoff. When I experienced a cash flow problem with my bumper sticker business, I was very short of cash for several weeks and had a sales force and bills to pay. However, I had formed a very strong relationship with my printer, and he knew that I wasn't going to cheat him on his bill. So he offered me extremely easy credit terms. This freed up cash to be used for other purposes. Even when my bill was overdue, he let me process more orders, knowing that when payment eventually came in he would receive his money right away. The strong rapport and deep trust that led to this arrangement were formed over months of working together, during which I had always treated him openly and honestly. In fact, we had been fair with each other. This man, Paul Hirsch, eventually wrote letters of recommendation that helped get me accepted in graduate school.

Get in the habit of establishing good ethics so that you don't think twice when a tantalizing though unethical opportunity comes your way. Almost always this type of decision involves a short-term gain but long-term negative consequences. There is an old saying that runs roughly like this: be careful whom you step on during your climb up the ladder of success, because you never know when you will meet them on your way down.

Trust and ethical standards are two elements of doing business that you should practice early in your business career. They are very important to you as a professional and to your own self-image. The importance of this aspect of the business world is now being recognized by some of the premier business schools in the country. At Yale it is a large factor in determining admissions, and Harvard makes a point of emphasizing in its catalog how highly it values an applicant's past ethical conduct.

If you're the type who is going to start your own business in college, you are obviously highly motivated, and in all likelihood you're going to be pretty successful in whatever career you choose. So keep in mind that even if you get the opportunity to sleaze a quick $1,000 or so, in comparison to your lifetime earnings you will have sold your integrity and self-worth for very little. I hope that you have enough on the ball that the idea of having to make money dishonestly is more of an insult than a temptation. You will learn, if you are one of the lucky ones, that there is more to life than just money.

Patience

Finally I want to pass on one of the most important pieces of advice in this chapter. BE PATIENT! Success rarely comes overnight, and if you're starting your *first* business, overnight success is even rarer. If you firmly believe you have a market for whatever product or service you are providing, stick it out at least one semester. Most real-life businesses can go two or three years before they turn a profit. Three or four months, then, is not much time to ask you to give your venture to make a profit. Always remember that, experience aside, if you fold a business, all the time, energy, and money that was put into it have been wasted. Why not give it another month and see if you can turn it all into success? Rome was not built in a day, and neither, for that matter, was General Motors. So why should you be the exception? However, don't stay with a venture that looks as if it is turning out to be a real dog. You have to use your own best judgment, but I urge you to ask yourself, "Have I been patient? Am I not asking too much of myself?"

So there you have it. If you've read this chapter carefully, you will be spared some of the more common stumbling blocks.

CHAPTER 9

Sample Business Startups

This chapter presents several businesses that can be, and have been, started by students and that are proven money makers. Although these businesses are discussed in detail, their implementation is left somewhat general on the assumption that half the fun of starting a business is making the decisions yourself. After all, if you are spoon-fed this stuff, how much can you really learn?

Frequently books of this nature tell the reader how to deal with separate issues but fail to tie the pieces together. In this chapter you and I will go through all the steps of starting up a business. Together we will plan, organize, and implement ventures that should minimally net $1,000 in profit and perhaps more. Much of what will be discussed has been pulled from concepts and discussions developed earlier in the book. Altogether, the discussions should give you the flavor of what starting your own business is all about.

College Publishing

The first business we are going to start together is a college publication. There are many different types of publications, such as sports programs, town guides for new students, coupon books, and school calendars. One particularly successful publication has been the student directory. This is a magazine (usually 8½ by 11 inches) that lists every student's name, school address, and phone number (some even give each student's mailbox number). They are distributed, usually free, to all students. Publications such as these are media vehicles that a local advertiser can use to reach the college market.

The Concept

In college, most youth-directed publications follow the same business principles; only the content or editorial matter changes. My expertise in this area lies in having run my own publishing company, which published soccer programs for several institutions. Constantly competing for advertising dollars, I got to know the essentials of the business. If you are interested in publishing, and your school already has a student directory or sports program, resort back to "need perception." Think of another publication that students would read with enthusiasm, and go out and publish it. When you read this chapter, you will see that it actually isn't that hard. (You also get to see your name in print as the publisher!)

Essentially, what is involved with starting a publication is to provide a link between your customers (the advertisers who provide you with revenues) and your clients (the students who use your publication, which you provide as a service). If the advertisers (customers) know that the students are using your publication and will see their message (advertisement), they will gladly pay money for the use of that advertising space.

There are four main areas where you may have problems. First, you could have difficulty obtaining the necessary advertising support for your costs and profit expectations. Inadequate advertising response is usually caused by a late start in selling ads, improper sales presentations, or lack of diligence. Of the three, lack of diligence is usually the most common. Selling usually encompasses a little rejection along the way, and some people just don't have the stomach for it.

Also, you could get a lousy printer who produces less than adequate quality and find that poor reproduction of ads turns away future prospective advertisers.

Third, the ad that appears in your directory may turn out to be different from the ad copy the advertiser gave you. If that sounds hard to do, you would be amazed at how unreadable some of the ad copy that you will receive can be. Small businesses rarely have professional advertising designed for them and instead usually scribble something barely legible on a piece of paper. The typesetter does the best he or she can, but mistakes do sometimes appear.

The fourth area where you can hit a snag is getting support from the school. School support is important in the effort to get permission to distribute. If students can't get your publication, they just won't read it. No readership translates into no ads.

So, if you keep an eye on these areas, you are on your way to making some money.

Planning

There are essentially two parts to starting a business: (1) market preparation and research and (2) the implementation. To get your directory off the ground, first do a little market research that will ideally tell (1) whether your publication can successfully enter the college publishing market, and (2) just how monetarily successful you can be.

This includes getting some ideas of cost and revenues as well as an idea of who and what the competition is. As far as your publication is concerned, these are the basic areas that you need to research:

- See the school administration to make sure you can distribute your product (publication).
- Get cost estimates.
- See who and what the competition is and what their rates are.
- Do some financial analysis and research that puts all the numbers together to see what the profit potential is.

When all the data and information are gathered, put them into a two- or three-page business plan. With these four areas covered, implementation should run smoothly.

Estimating Printing Costs

The first step after talking to the school administration is to get some estimates on the biggest expense, printing. In order to get an idea of the cost of your publication, a printer needs to know your specifications. Your specs include the number and size of pages, the type of paper (stock), the number of copies of the directory to be printed, and the number of colors in which it will be printed. Usually, good old black and white is more than adequate.

The first thing you need to do is to figure out how much space you need for editorial content. Advertising space should be just under 50 percent of the total number of pages in the book. Thus, if your book is 24 pages, anywhere from 10 to 13 pages of advertising would be a good showing. Even eight or nine pages shows a strong effort. The total number of pages must be divisible by four because most small books are printed in large sheets called "signatures," which when folded in half make four pages. As an example, look at a newspaper. As you will see, the other half of the sheet of paper that has page 1 is always the last page. The only differences between a newspaper and your publication are that yours is smaller and most newspapers are not stapled (bound) in the middle the way many publications are. Take three sheets of paper, fold each in half, and make a mini program or what is called a "dummy." It will help you considerably in communicating with your printer.

The Selection

Now that you have a rough idea of what you want from a printer, the selection process begins. The best place to start is the school publications department. Its staff constantly asks local printers to submit bids on various projects and should well be able to provide you with a sizable list of reasonably priced printers who don't skimp on quality. Ask from three to five printers to submit bids. It has been my experience that printing estimates should be divided into two segments: (1) layout and artwork costs and (2) press time and paper costs (or what it costs to print your directory from "camera ready" copy). A printer can make a substantial profit in artwork and typesetting charges, so it makes sense to shop around. You might also check a typesetting specialist who does just typesetting and get his or her rates. The telephone book Yellow Pages is a good source for these names. And let's not forget the publications department. It should also be invited to give an estimate for its services.

PRINTING CHECKLIST

Cover

Cost of plain cover stock	$_____
Cost of coated (glossy) cover stock	$_____
Cost of ordinary paper stock (for entire publication)	$_____
Cost of coated (glossy) stock (for entire publication)	$_____

Printing run

Cost of required printing run	$_____
Cost of required printing run less 500 copies	$_____
Cost of required printing run plus 500 copies	$_____
Cost of required printing run plus 1,000 copies	$_____
Cost of required printing run plus four pages (one signature)	$_____
Cost of required printing run less four pages (one signature)	$_____

Colors

Cost for printing in black and white	$_____
Cost for printing in two colors	$_____
Cost for four-color printing (very expensive)	$_____

Miscellaneous

Cost for each halftone (photograph)	$_____
Cost for typesetting per page	$_____
Cost of a bleed	$_____
Cost of a reverse	$_____
Cost of binding and stitching	$_____

When you are done with this section of research, you should have a good idea of who your printer will be and who will be doing your artwork. If you can't decide, have the closest estimators rebid on the project after telling them the lowest current bid and see if anyone can shave another couple of dollars off the price. When you select a printer, get all the estimates in writing. My first experience with a printer was nothing short of disastrous because our costs were almost double the estimates and nothing was in writing. I wept all the way to the loan officer. The lesson stands, and I sincerely hope you can profit by it. This ensures that you do not find yourself with a 30- to 40-percent cost overrun. Explain to the printer that you can't possibly bring him any future business if you don't make a profit. How can you make a profit if your printer doesn't give you an accurate estimate of the printing costs so that you can set profitable rates? Logic like this can fail to penetrate only the densest of minds.

Competition

At this point I think it is time that we received more information about the competition. Your competition is anyone you are competing with for revenues from advertising sales. Who, then, is selling space for the same readership you are trying to reach—students)? Furthermore, what are they charging and what circulation do they claim for their advertisers? Are their rates cost-efficient? They may charge half your rates but only reach one-quarter of your anticipated circulation. There is a very simple formula for calculating advertising cost efficiency, called cost per thousand, or CPM. The formula looks like this:

$$\text{Cost} \div \text{Circulation (in thousands)} = \text{CPM}$$

For example, if you had a circulation of 10,000 readers and charged $20 (an absurdly low price), your CPM would be:

$$\$20.00 \div 10 = \$2.00 \text{ cost per thousand}$$

This means it costs the advertiser $2 to reach every 1,000 readers.

When you have all the information on your competitors along with their rates, you can get a good idea of the range of prices. Do some figuring on everyone's CPM and see who is reasonable and who may be in danger of exposure to competition by overcharging. If you choose to be aggressive, you will probably want to set your rates toward the low end of the spectrum. However, the costs will have a lot to say about where you set your rates.

Let's now proceed to the final part of your market research, which is the financial analysis of the numbers you have gathered. This determines your projected profits and is a method of determining your rates.

Number Crunching

Financial analysis can be as simple or as complicated as you want to make it. Essentially, the purpose is to supply yourself with information.

First, let us direct ourselves toward costs, specifically printing costs. By now you should have some estimates from your prospective printers, and the costs will be broken down as far as possible. This enables you to see the whole picture and decide where you can cut corners. In addition, it lets you play one printer off another by allowing you to compare various components of your project as well as the whole sum. For instance, you may find that printer A charges $300 for artwork and $3,200 for printing services, whereas printer B charges $500 for artwork and only $2,000 for printing. Obviously, you would attempt to contract the artwork to printer A and the presswork to printer B. Realistically, this cannot always be done, as many printers will throw you a lowball figure on artwork just to get your printing work. Naturally, these printers are reluctant to part with the lower-priced of their two services if they can't get you to use their higher-priced serivce, which is the bread-and-butter item on their menu. But if you look thoroughly enough, you will be rewarded for your efforts.

Breaking down your printing bid as far as possible also lets you see what extra costs would be incurred should you find yourself in the enviable position of having to add additional pages as a result of enthusiastic advertising response. In other words, you want to know what it is going to cost your company to add another four-page signature to your printing specifications should advertising response be so good that you need to expand to accommodate demand. You may find that coated (glossy) paper is only a minimum surcharge over the regular paper stock. Going with a glossy stock might be a smart move because it enhances your publication considerably and makes next year's publication all that much easier to sell. You want as many options on your printing as possible. I caution you against consistently selecting the cheapest option because later you will be setting rates, much of which is influenced by costs. You want to leave some room for economizing on your publication in case advertising results fall short of expectations.

Now you have to estimate the other, extra costs, which might collectively be called overhead. Gas expenses, telephone expenses, your salary (if you have the cash flow to pay yourself), and advertising sales commissions are all items you want to consider. It is going to be extremely difficult to estimate all those expenses precisely. So when you do, it is wise to gauge them on the high side. For instance, if you already have a phone service with virtually unlimited local use, you will perhaps have no additional phone expense; but just to be conservative, you may want to estimate $20 per month for business phone expenses. Once you have figured these costs, you will have a good picture of what kind of advertising revenues you need to break even. You may even wish to add another 10 to 20 percent for hidden costs, which undoubtedly will surface.

Half the financial analysis is now complete. Let's suppose that you have figured you will have a total printing cost of $2,000, which could be trimmed by $500 should you find yourself having to slash costs. Also, let's figure that you have $560 of overhead, which is broken down as follows:

Phone expense	$ 50
Car and gas	40
Ad sales commissions (15%)	300
Office supplies	20
Miscellaneous	100
Stationery supplies (rate cards, etc.)	50
TOTAL	560

This means we can anticipate roughly $2,600 (remember to round off to the higher number) of expenses. Keep in mind that $300 of your overhead is commission, which you yourself will be earning if you're selling the advertising, and is not an out-of-pocket cash expense.

SAMPLE BUSINESS STARTUPS

Revenues

It is now time to start thinking about your advertising rates. When setting your rates, first evaluate the competition's rates in terms of both total dollars and CPM (cost per thousand). Then find out how much revenue per page you need to at least break even ($2,600 ÷ 10 ad pages = $260). Because this is a first-time publication, you may very well elect to follow an aggressive strategy and set your rates on the low end of the rate spectrum. At the same time, you want to keep an eye on costs. Setting rates involves a lot of trial and error because, obviously, you want revenues to exceed costs as well as to have your rates be competitive. Assume you want to make a 30-percent profit on costs, which would be .30 × $2,600 = $750. This means revenues have to be $2,600 + $750 = $3,350. If you are planning a 20-page publication of which 10 pages are intended for advertising space, you want to get roughly $335 per page in revenues ($3,350 ÷ 10). Some pages will be more (the back cover usually gets a healthy surcharge because it is usually the highest-visibility spot for an advertising message), and some pages will be less. However, don't let a page go for less than $260 (costs ÷ 10 revenue-producing pages); this is in effect selling at a loss, and absolutely no one is in business to sell for less than cost.

You are going to find that because you have a first-year publication, most merchants will only commit to a small purchase. Don't assume that because a full page might go for $300 a half page goes for $150. Not so. You charge a surcharge. As far as I know, there is no rule of thumb for this type of publication (low circulation, college audience), but the rate structure I used was as follows:

Full page	$350
Half page	200
Quarter page	125
Back cover	400
Inside covers	375

Note that there is roughly a 10-percent surcharge for each smaller size. That is to say that a *half*-page ad is half the cost of a full page plus 10 percent. In this case, $350 ÷ 2 + $35 = $192.50, which I rounded up to an even $200. This means half-page ads are bringing in $400 per page and quarter-page ads are fetching *$500* per page!

Now guess what size is going to be your hottest sales item? You guessed it! The quarter-page ads, because they are the lowest-ticket item on your rate card. It is extremely important in this business that you understand your numbers.

Because it is your first year, you will in all likelihood cut some deals with local merchants in order to get their business. Businesspeople love to think they talked you into a price break, and it never hurts to try to haggle with them as a last resort if they reject your original invitation to place an ad. Eight out of ten will continue to say no, but those two who finally do agree to place an advertisement will in all probability put a couple of hundred dollars in your pocket.

Incremental Costs

What happens if advertising response is fantastic and instead of selling $3,600 of advertising you end up selling $4,300 of ads? How much of the extra $700 is profit? Well, so long as you didn't sell so much advertising that it has become necessary to add pages, the whole $700 is yours.

Have fun in Bermuda!

Think about it. How much real cost do you incur by selling the extra ads? None, since you are dealing primarily with one big fixed cost—your printing bill. Sure, it varies, but not by very much. Even if you throw another four pages into a 20-page publication, you will incur about a 15-percent total increase in cost. But in return you should expect an increase of 20 to 30 percent in revenues.

You must spend a couple of hours crunching numbers to familiarize yourself with the financial aspect of your venture. Particularly important is comparing different cost relationships. For instance, if you cut circulation by 30 percent, by what amount will your printing costs drop? If you add another four-page signature, how many ads will you have to sell in order to justify the extra printing and typesetting cost? These and the many other cost relationships are important for you to know before you will truly know the financial mechanism of your company. If you really want to be thorough, do a "what if" sensitivity analysis on your costs versus revenues. *What* would happen to costs *if* revenues went up by 10, 20, or 50 percent? *What* would revenues have to be *if* circulation were doubled and increased printing costs 20 percent?

By the end of this first stage, which is collectively called market research, you should have a feel for what you are getting involved in. You know the competition, and you have a feel for the numbers and what you stand to make or lose.

Now it's time to put together all of the numbers and other pieces of market research you have gathered in order to make them work for you. I must assume that all of your numbers look promising and that you have decided to make a go of it. For this example, your firm will be called Publications Unlimited.

Determining a Strategy

Formulating the strategy is the most essential part of the startup. How are you going to get advertisers? You may have answered this question when you set your rates. Your rates tell whether you have chosen an aggressive pricing strategy or a middle-of-the-road approach. Rates are one of the key components of your overall strategy, because they are a critical factor in determining how successful you are in obtaining sales.

There are no predetermined rules for setting rates. However, I think it makes sense when first starting out to be aggressive. A low price is one of the best means of obtaining sales. This means you must set your rates at a competitive level, which means they are lower than or nearly equal to your competition's rates. This will enable you to make the selling point that your media vehicle (your publication) is a more economical method of reaching the college market. Consequently, your competition's prices, in both actual dollars and CPMs, have a great deal to say about how you set your rates. As I said before, when setting rates you must have a knowledge of (1)

167

your competition's prices, (2) your competition's CPMs, and (3) the amount of revenue each of your advertising pages must produce in order for you to break even.

One last area to discuss again is rate imposting. Rate imposting is the additional charge you set over the proportionate share of a full-page ad rate. As I said earlier, a half-page ad is seldom charged at half the cost of a full-page ad, but rather it has a surcharge. Because my publishing firm was dealing with many advertisers who mainly wanted to demonstrate their support for the school, my strategy was to add large imposts to the rates. My rates and impost surcharges looked like this:

Size	Actual rate	Percent of full page	Impost charge
Full page	$300	—	—
Half page (50%)	$200	66%	33%
Quarter page (25%)	$125	41%	50%

Because most advertisers who merely want to show their support for a school take the smallest ad possible, I made sure that I got a nice surcharge on that size. Strategically this made the most sense. A quarter-page at this price results in a healthy $500-per-page revenue figure (4 × $125). It never bothered me when advertisers went for the $125 cheapie because I knew I was making a terrific return on each page of quarter-page ads.

Plans

What are you going to do *now* to put the wheels into motion? Your plan should state such things as

1. Receive bids from at least five printers within two weeks' time.
2. Obtain a list of school suppliers (prospective advertisers) by a certain date.
3. Have business card printed within ten days.

You may wish to set plans in two- or three-week increments so that you can get a new perspective on how things are progressing every time you sit down to review what has been finished and what needs to be done next.

The final step in implementation is writing down all of the aforementioned in a condensed two- to four-page business plan (larger if you are tackling a more grandiose undertaking). This document gives you (and your partner, if you take on one) something to refer to when the time comes. If nothing else, it serves as a record of your undertaking whether you are successful or not. At the end of your sales cycle it is often quite helpful to refer back to your business plan. A sales cycle in this case is the amount of time it takes to sell out one publication. You can then make the necessary improvements and changes that will make your next directory even better.

The Busy Work

Now that the planning and research stages are done, it is time to make your business an actual entity. Several things need to be done. This busy work is what has to get done in order to get the business up and running. First, you need to rent a post office address in the name of your firm so that you have an address for people who need to send you ad copy, bills, or payments. Of course, you could just have everyone send it to you in care of your local address, but more often than not this method reeks of unprofessionalism. For a mere $10, a post office box is certainly worthwhile.

Such things as getting a phone, filing for a tax number, and opening a bank account are all necessary duties. One last task in the order of busy work might be to order printed rate cards and business cards. If you are looking for the absolute minimum in startup costs, business cards could be eliminated and rate cards can be typed and mimeographed rather than printed; but there is a trade-off between costs saved and credibility forsaken. Business cards don't really cost that much ($15 to $25), and they do enhance the professional image of your company. Don't get me wrong—business cards aren't going to conjure up images of your being president of some miniconglomerate. However, they do tell potential advertisers that you are sincere enough about your business to invest some money in business cards. There are practical considerations as well. They are good for providing basic information such as name, address, phone number, and zip code, all in one place. You can use business cards to your best advantage by trading them with your prospective advertisers, so that you have basic information about them. In addition, many people choose simply to use business cards as advertising copy, which is another good reason to get everyone's card.

Rate cards are another element of printing needs and can be either typed and mimeographed sheets or professional-looking 3-by-5-inch cards. The more professional-looking card is preferable. It should cost only $30 to $40, and, once again, it bolsters your image and your credibility. On the other hand, mimeographed rate sheets only cost 5 cents each.

Regardless of your selection, there are certain pieces of information that should be included in your rate card. Obviously your rates are the most important piece of information, but items such as the estimated circulation, the date of the publication's release, and additional charges for typesetting services must also be included.

Sales

The pivot point of starting your publishing venture is obtaining revenue—SALES. Sales, when properly planned, can be doubly effective, and planning, for all its benefits, doesn't take that much time. Anyone who blindly goes out and knocks on doors trying to sell advertising for a directory, or anything else, is not only wasting a lot of time but is probably acquiring a negative image of what selling can be. I know, because I've done both.

In planning your advertising sales campaign, you should first put together a list of advertising prospects, those merchants who you feel are inclined to advertise in a publication such as yours. A good way of getting a list of prospects to start with is to obtain the names of vendors that the school does business with, such as food caterers and oil suppliers.

This list can in many cases be obtained from the school purchasing agent. Another good source of information for advertising prospects is advertisers in existing student-oriented publications. Get some school publications like the newspaper and make a list of all the advertisers. You might further identify prospects by asking yourself who could stand to benefit from reaching your market (need perception). Obviously a Rolls Royce dealership won't get a whole lot of student business, but a pizza shop might. Since your directory is for a college or university, local bars are ideal prospects. Banks have always been a good source for me, because they usually have a budget specifically set up for this kind of thing. You will find that roughly half of your clients will advertise merely to show support for the school. Often there is a school connection, such as an alumnus or alumna or an unknown relationship to the school.

Selling Points and Your Distinctive Features

Once you have a prospect list, group the prospects geographically and by need. Now make two lists of your selling points, one containing general benefits of advertising and the other listing benefits that are unique to your publication. The point of the first list of selling points is to convince your prospect that he or she needs to advertise. The second list is to convince him or her to advertise with you!

From experience, let me tell you that the former is by far the more difficult. Many people have trouble visualizing the benefits of advertising. If advertising were as simple as putting an ad in a publication and getting business the next day, people would never go out of business. Small businesses tend to view advertising with less sophistication and understanding. Getting the message out encompasses coordination of many advertisements that as a whole serve to bring business through the door. One ad just won't do it. How is anyone going to know about XYZ store if it doesn't advertise? Word-of-mouth advertising just isn't that easy.

Students are a good market for your clients to sell to because although they are cost-conscious, they have tremendous amounts of disposable income. A great selling point that I was known to dangle in front of merchants from time to time was a rough guess at the total expenditures by all our students. If you have 1,000 students and figure they each spend $15 per week on purchases, that means $15,000 per week per 1,000 students. Now why, Mr. Merchant, can't you have a piece of that?

Because you don't advertise!

Some Selling Tips

When you make your first sales calls, there are several things to keep in mind. You must have an attitude that you probably don't have now. In your everyday life you approach everything with the expectation of succeeding. If you don't pass an exam, you are naturally disappointed. If you don't make the team, you feel rejected. If you are kept back a year in school you feel a sense of failure. In selling, however, rejection is part of the game. There is absolutely no one who makes a sale every time he or she calls on a prospect. The people who are successful in sales are those who can keep their spirits up and keep right on talking to more prospects, even after being rejected. I can't tell you how many guys I knew in college who got good ideas, researched them, developed them, and when the time came to sell got dismayed after the first couple of prospect calls. On the flip side of the coin, those who were the most diligent in the sales effort always had the most successful businesses.

Probably one of the most useful pieces of information I ever learned when I went to work selling for The Boeing Company was the concept of aiming for the top. You don't want to talk to the clerk; you want to talk to the manager. If given a further choice, you would really rather talk to the owner. I don't know how many times I got into a long pitch about the merits of advertising in my soccer programs with some bimbo who had absolutely no authority to sign a contract. The higher up the organization you go, the better your chances of success are. This includes the Mom and Pop shop as well as the big corporate campus advertisers like Coca-Cola and Budweiser. The manager or the owner is the person you should target. You know he or she can make a decision. If sent down a level, at least it's to a decision maker. But if you start off with a non–decision maker, it is insulting to that person if you decide to go over his or her head. Someone on a lower level may not be able to sign a contract with you, but he or she sure as hell can see to it that you don't get that order. The basic point is that if you can find a way to start at the top without antagonizing, or even encountering, those at the lower levels, it is preferable to do so.

Protect-Expand

At this point you have successfully published your first directory. You have established a good rapport with the school and have a solid base of advertisers. It is dangerously easy now to sit back, count your profits, and consider the job done. Beware! Attitudes like that lead to an erosion of your advertising base. Rather than the job's being finished, the cycle has now just begun and you must think ahead. Keep in mind that the more successful your directory is, the more money you can sell the business for when the eventual day of graduation comes and you step out into the big, bad real world.

You must look at your product and think of how you can improve upon its design, layout, and other features. Ask some of your classmates what they liked most about it and what they liked least and see how you can turn these suggestions into helpful improvements. One reason for doing this is that it shows the school that you are genuinely interested in improving your product, which has its name on it. It also demonstrates to the advertisers that you believe in quality.

Another area that you must think about is improving your rapport with your customers/advertisers. Advertisers who address the school market typically never see the guy who sold them the ad after the day they paid their bill. Consequently, the publisher who makes a concerted effort to get to know his or her advertisers *after* the bills have been paid usually gets a large increase in loyalty to the publication. Many people, especially students, are too shortsighted to think of laying groundwork today for tomorrow's advertising sale.

Not only is a successful publishing venture possible while you are at school, but it can also be amazingly fun. Any time you find a situation that can be fun, profitable, and a learning experience, all in one, give it a try. After all, opportunities like that don't come down the pike that often. Even if you don't make bundles of money, the experience, poise, and street knowledge that you will have gained will ultimately result in a payoff.

Car Wash and Protection Service

The Four P's

Product. This venture is another service-oriented business that requires a minimal up-front investment and has the potential of returning to you a very good profit. For example, for a couple of hundred dollars' worth of materials you could very easily gross over $6,000. This product is deliberately called a Car Wash and Protection Service rather than a plain old boring car wash business for the simple reason that you aren't selling a car wash—the product—you are selling a whole concept of what your service does. This business doesn't just wash cars, it cleans them, shines them, makes them lustrous, protects them, and adds to their bodies' life. In short, it is not just an indulgence for car owners, it's an investment.

The point here is that you are selling an image just the way Detroit is when Chrysler ads stress the "rich Corinthian leather." The actual engines among the different manufacturers are similar, and in fact many different models use the same engines. What is different is the image. It is this image that a car wash and protection business plays upon and is what allows you to get away with charging $50 plus per job. Not that it isn't worth it, mind you, but a car wash only charges $5 to $10. The difference is the perceived quality that one projects through using advanced polishes, compounds, and waxes and the way that quality is communicated to car owners.

Many people, especially those with expensive cars like a BMW or Mercedes, think of their car as an extension of their own personality. Some people buy Datson 280ZX cars and some people buy Cadillac Sevilles. For each, the car represents something different. Both cars get you from A to B in relatively the same degree of comfort and at about the same speed. What both sets of people have in common is that they value the image of a high-prestige car. These people will usually pay a premium price for a premium protection for their premium car.

On the other hand, a person with a beat-up 1966 Chevy isn't likely to be very interested in any kind of cosmetic improvement on his or her car. The car is viewed more as basic transportation than as a dream come true. Thus, the importance of market segmentation is crucial with this business. Your market is not all people with cars. It is people who either have expensive cars or place a great deal of value on the appearance of their cars. Professional businesspeople and salespeople are likely to fall into the latter category whether they tool around in a Porsche or a Dodge Aries.

As you may have gathered, selecting the right target market is very important in this business. There are some generalizations about preferred targets that include expensive cars, particularly foreign cars; wealthy neighborhoods; office parks and people selling their cars who want to improve the resale value. One thing all these groups have in common is that the cosmetic appearance of their cars is very important.

Promotion.   Promoting your service is one of the key ways to get customers because this is a product that often sells itself. The best promotion is often a free demonstration. More than one enterprising student has given a free demonstration to a car or truck rental fleet to end up with a multi-thousand-dollar contract. If you choose to go after industrial clients aggressively, I would highly recommend this method. Make sure that you do a bang-up job on your demonstration, because if the job is superb you probably will have the business. If you do a lot of demonstrations, make sure that you pick a good car that will stress your workmanship rather than a car with a fading paint job that no amount of work will cure.

Two other forms of promotion are flyers and brochures. Flyers cost roughly a nickel apiece to produce, but you have to distribute 300 to 400 to get a single sale, so the cost is $15 to $20 per job. Brochures cost more but are generally more effective. You can leave them with people who either aren't in or might need your service but not just now. Remember, you will encounter a lot of rejection, but it doesn't necessarily mean people don't want a beautiful car. They just don't need one now for any number of reasons. It could be as simple as the fact that they just recently had it done.

Place.   Some places are better than others for giving demonstrations and selling the service. Shopping malls, though a wide variety of people pass through them who aren't in your target market, do have the advantage of high volume. Moreover, a demonstration given in the middle of the mall parking lot gets a lot of attention quickly. The successful owner of a car waxing business, John Lyons of Newport Beach, California, highly recommends using shopping malls as an efficient way of doing business. One trick that John recommends is doing only half your demonstration car to show a before-and-after effect.

Office complexes are another location that have a large volume of cars whose owners are consistent with your target market—businesspeople and salespeople. Moreover, these cars will usually be there the entire day, giving you plenty of time to do a thorough job. The trick is to get to the parking lot early in the morning, park your half-done demonstration car in prominent view, and approach owners as they arrive. The chapter on selling should help you with your actual sales approach. Don't forget to bring brochures or flyers, if you have them, to give to those prospects who are interested but not immediately in need.

Price.   The best way to price your car wash and protection service is to do a quick analysis and see what the competition is charging. You can do this in a half hour over the phone or in an afternoon if you go in person. Knowing what the local competition charges gives you some guidelines by which to price your service. If you want to be aggressive, you will charge less and use that as a selling point. If you are willing to take a chance (risk), you will charge as much or more than the competition in exchange for a higher profit. After all, if it doesn't work you can always lower your price later. I also suggest, if you go after some industrial volume users like car rental services, that you give an enticing volume discount. These people have profit goals to meet, and you can easily price yourself out of the market despite the fact that you have a product that they need.

Keeping Records

Besides your normal accounting records, it is vitally important to keep customer records. Those records allow you to contact customers after three to four months so that you can reprotect their car. Repeat business can eventually become a substantial part of your sales.

John Lyons estimates that 70 percent of the customers whom you keep track of will be repeat customers. This means if you grind for three months or so you will have acquired a base of customers. They will keep coming back to you if you stimulate their needs by sending a reminder or phoning them after several months. It works for dentists, and it can work for you.

Another reason for keeping a book on your customers is that should you decide to sell your business those records are worth a great deal. Because anyone could start a car protection and wash service, there appears to be no reason for someone to buy *your* business. The distinctive asset of your business, which they can't get anywhere else, is that list of customers—ready-made. All the hard work of face-to-face selling is done. Moreover, if you have taken it one step further and used an appointment book to schedule customers, you can promise the new owners of your business immediate sales tomorrow. That customer list *is* your business, and with it you can command a great deal more money for your hard-earned efforts.

How the Process Works

As soon as a car is driven out of the showroom and exposed to the elements, the car's exterior begins a slow process of decay. The combination of sun, salt, water, and pollution gradually takes its toll on a car, and over the years the paint begins to fade and the body starts to rust. That is, unless the owner uses your service.

Car wax forms a protective coating over the car's body to seal out the elements that damage the finish. This is the essential concept of the business. Thus, your service can be conceptualized as an investment whose return takes the form of a longer life expectancy of a better-looking car.

There are varying degrees of quality in waxes and also of doing the job. For instance, merely waxing a car is one thing, but washing and Simonizing a car is very different altogether and yields a higher price. Here are the basic products that you need to get your business started.

Cleaning polish. This is one step up from regular soap and water. It contains abrasives and solvents that add shine to the paint. These abrasives and solvents are a selling tool, as they do a better job than soap and water.

Rubbing compound. This is a stronger substance than the cleaning polish and should be used when there is hard-to-get-at dirt (or once a year at most). Rubbing compound can wear down a car's finish, so overusing it defeats the purpose of your service.

Interior cleaning products. While the outside dries from the cleaning with polish and/or rubbing compound, you are ready to begin the interior. The first step is vacuuming, which can be done either with your family or dorm vacuum and a lot of extension cords or with a portable car vacuum. If you're

178

really serious about this type of business I suggest that you invest in a car vacuum, since they are much more convenient and plug right into the cigarette lighter.

For cleaning leather upholstery, saddle soap works best. If you encounter vinyl upholstery (or roof), you will need a vinyl cleaner. This can be found in most automotive supply stores and supermarkets. Afterward you may wish to apply a vinyl protectant such as Armorall, which is the most common. Window cleaners are also a must and can be found in any supermarket.

Exterior enhancements. Up to this point you haven't really done anything much different from any other car wash service. Now come the enhancements. First, a high-quality chrome polish shines all outside metal on bumpers, hub caps, front grilles, and door handles. Your customers will notice your attention to this kind of detail. The next product is a Simonized wax, of which there are many. Du Pont is a leader in this industry, but there are other manufacturers as well. It would be wise to get in touch with several automobile supply stores and get a few opinions on which makes the best product. Finally, you may add a protection-plus treatment, which is applied over the wax and doubles its life. You definitely want to charge more if you elect to make this part of your service, because not only is it another product you have to pay for, it allows double the amount of time before you will see this customer again. Consequently, keep in mind that there is an opportunity cost.

One final piece of advice: be sure that the towels you use are soft and will maximize the shine and luster on the car. Some towels are much softer and better suited for this purpose.

Conclusion

Car wash and protection is a very labor-intensive service-oriented business that does not require a large up-front capital investment. The bare minimum of materials could probably be gotten for $40 to $50 or, if you wanted to go all out, perhaps as much as $80. If you choose to get an automobile vacuum cleaner, it could be several hundred dollars more, so you must decide whether it is worth it. Because there is a minimum of variable cost associated with this business (the cost per car in materials is probably less than $8), there is a very high contribution margin (difference between the cost and what you charge). This means that by doing just eight cars at $50 each you can cover the cost of a vacuum cleaner ($50 − $8 variable cost = $42 × 8 cars = $336). Moreover, with this kind of contribution margin you need to do only three or four cars per week (one every other day) to make this a financially rewarding venture.

Pizza Delivery Service

Since I've referred so often to an evening study hour pizza delivery service, surely you did not think I would neglect to go into more detail. A pizza delivery business is one of the most educational and profitable businesses a student can run. It does not require a great deal of capital, although it does in most cases require a car. This is a service business, so you are incurring labor costs plus the cost of goods sold, but the initial capital outlay is minimal. With a sound marketing implementation strategy and with a little perseverance, it is quite possible to net several thousand dollars in a school year. What's more, if you budget your time right and delegate most of the manual labor, there will not be a tremendous drain on your time.

Operations

After checking to be sure that this need is not already being met, the first thing you need to do is to procure a reliable supplier. There are three things that you can offer your supplier—high volume, cash, and reliability. You should use them as leverage to get the most favorable terms you can. If you can guarantee a certain number of pizzas per night, he or she can start preparing them ahead of time in the slow business period in the middle to late afternoon before the dinner rush. This allows your supplier to smooth out the work flow. Also, because of the high volume, your supplier orders more flour, tomatoes, and other ingredients and gets a better quantity discount from his or her suppliers.

You also offer cash. That is to say, you collect cash and therefore can pay cash at the end or even the beginning of the night. However, you may elect to establish a credit arrangement whereby you pay weekly or monthly. When you initially contact pizza store owners it is better to set up cash terms so that the owner gives you a better price. After all, you are an unknown quantity and if you ask for too much up front you may not generate any interest in your business. If you eventually generate a sizable volume, the supplier will probably be more than interested in giving you credit in order to keep you as a customer.

Reliability becomes even more important after the relationship has been formed and the pizza store owner has had a chance to see what a consistently profitable customer you are. As the owner gets used to his or her newly found profit machine (you), he or she will be more and more likely to give you better service and price. Remember, direct costs are the name of the game. The lower your pizza cost is, the higher your margin will be and the more formidable an opponent you will be to a competitor.

When you have suppliers bid on your business, you too should look for price, reliability, and eventual credit terms. Price and reliability are especially important. If your supplier cops out on you with a 100-pizza delivery, there aren't many suppliers who are going to be able to meet your demand on short notice. Price is important because of the need for low direct costs. Credit terms are nice but not crucial in the early days of the venture because the keys to sales and market share in this business are price and reliability.

Marketing the Four P's

Product.   Make no mistake about it, the product you are selling is not pizza. It is convenience, affordability, and reliability. Pizza is sold everywhere, including the school snack bar. A dorm-to-dorm, door-to-door delivery service is successful because everyone knows that a pizza delivery person will be around at a certain time on the publicized days. That is why they stay in their rooms and continue studying instead of going out and getting a pizza themselves. As you will probably agree, there is nothing nicer than a munchie break when you have to put in a long evening of study. Thus, you must be reliable, though it may take a couple of weeks to develop a reputation of reliability. However, once you have it, you will be a welcome face at the late evening hour.

Price.　Your price should be roughly the same as the competition's, which more often than not will be the local pizza shop. However, should a door-to-door competitor enter into things, the best way to keep your market share is to compete on price, assuming you were there first and have a higher volume. This gets back to the earlier discussion regarding cost and volume. The higher the volume, the lower your direct pizza cost should be, and accordingly, the lower your price can be. If you have a lower direct cost than your competitor, you can sell at a price at which he or she loses money on every sale made and you still make a small amount.

For instance, if you pay a direct cost of $1 per pizza (because you have high volume) and your competitor pays $1.20 per pizza, you can charge $1.15 and still make money. Your competitor, on the other hand, will lose 5 cents per pizza if he or she matches your price and even more if he or she chooses to undercut you.

Place.　The method of distribution should be as close to the consumer as you can get. If the school rules allow you only into the front door of dorms, you go there and have your presence announced over the page system if there is one. Otherwise, stalk the halls and yell out a couple of times, "Fresh hot pizza." Be careful not to overstay your welcome and irritate studying students by your yelling. A couple of yells per hallway should be enough.

You should get a campus map, plot out your salespeople's routes, and calculate how long it takes them to go from dorm to dorm. They should always follow the same route so that they arrive at each dorm at approximately the same time.

Also, in order to be able to deliver your pizza piping hot, your salespeople will need insulated boxes to carry them around in. Large beer coolers are good for this, although you may want to experiment with extra insulation to keep the heat in longer. Once a pizza gets cold there isn't much demand for it. If you get a reputation for cold pizza, you are open to competition and declining sales.

Promotion. The best promotion is service and price. Otherwise you could try an initial poster and leaflet blitz coupled with a one- or two-week discount when you open your business. This lets everyone know your hours of delivery so that they can plan around your arrival. The initial discount is good for getting customers to try your service. Otherwise, general advertising and promotion expenses are unnecessary—one of the reasons this business can be so profitable. The less overhead you have, the more money you are going to make.

Expansion

The logic to this business is simple. The higher your volume, the lower your direct costs will be. The lower your direct costs, the more money you are going to make. Therefore, the more campuses you penetrate, the lower your unit pizza costs are going to be, and the more money you will make. Expansion can be tricky, though. You certainly don't want to get a student manager set up at another campus only to have him or her decide to do it on his or her own, but thank you for showing how to do it. In order to prevent this type of situation you have to set up controls.

If you are employing student managers and salespeople, you must cut them in on a piece of the action. This entails a commission structure that yields them an incentive return and also makes money for you. I recommend a graduated commission structure that pays them more per pizza at higher volumes than at lower volumes. This gives them incentive to sell more. The more you try to keep for yourself, the more likely they will be to quit or, more probably, to go out on their own.

The recommended approach to instituting controls is to make sure that all cash transactions with the supplier are made with you only. Your salespeople will have to go back to the supplier periodically throughout the night to restock. If you have the supplier keep count of the number of pizzas that go out the door, you will know how much money was collected by multiplying the number of pizzas by your selling price. This stops anyone from skimming money off the top.

The best and most profitable pizza delivery operation that I ever knew of was run by a student at Babson who allowed the individual campus managers complete decision-making freedom on their own campuses. The philosophy was that they knew their own market better than anyone else, so they selected the delivery times, routes, and marketing plan. What they didn't select was the supplier, since that was how the owner kept tabs on how many pizzas were being sold and the corresponding revenues his managers should be reporting.

Conclusion

I like this business for several reasons. It is simple, it doesn't take a lot of up-front cash, and it makes money. It gives great hands-on management and marketing experience, and finally it can be set up with a minimal drain on your time if you delegate properly. If your local pizza shop already delivers without charge, you can just substitute another food/munchie product for pizza. The concept remains the same: the more you put into it, the more money you will make.

T-Shirt Business

A T-shirt business probably won't make you a campus millionaire, but it is one of the simplest enterprises to run. You can make some quick and painless bucks. The fundamental concept is to imprint or silk screen a logo or message on a

T-shirt to appeal to your target market. There already are companies that make college promotional items such as pens, running shorts, cups, and even T-shirts. The opportunity that they leave you to take advantage of is the fact that generally these companies only go after the mass market and leave isolated niches that you can address selectively.

At Yale, for example, the college book store (known in New Haven as the Co-op) sells items that only say "Yale" or "Yale University." This leaves many opportunities for entrepreneurial types. In 1982, for instance, a second-year student at the Yale School of Management (SOM), Stu Patterson, saw an unfilled need for SOM T-shirts and quickly moved to meet it. It only took a little time and practically no up-front capital, yet it netted him several hundred dollars in profits.

Likewise, a previously mentioned student entrepreneur, Steve Muller, saw a need at the NCAA (Division III) soccer championships that were held in Wellesley, Massachusetts, in 1978. Steve and a fraternity brother made several hundred T-shirts with the NCAA logo and date of the championship game imprinted on the front. Their rationale was that the families and fans of the participating schools would eagerly buy a souvenir of the championship. The hunch paid off, and Steve and his partner sold several hundred shirts in a matter of five hours. The point I'm trying to make is that if you are careful about the message you put on your T-shirt (select your target market carefully), you can make several hundred dollars with a minimal amount of time invested.

Getting Started

The first thing to do is to see or call several printers and silk-screening businesses to get the best price you can manage. During this phase of the startup you want to know such things as the cost of just a plain unprinted shirt (this determines whether you supply the shirts or not), the cost of switching to different-colored shirts (so that you can offer a selection), the amount of time from when an order is placed to expected delivery, and finally whether there is a volume discount. Once you know your costs and your options, such as colors, volume

185

discounts, and the like, you are ready to begin your marketing plan.

The Four P's

Product.   The product here is not a plain T-shirt that people can buy anywhere. The product is a message that happens to be on a T-shirt. It could, for that matter, be on a pen, a cigarette lighter, a scarf, or any other item that is used as a promotional tool. Since this is the case, the message is your distinctive competence and thus all-important. It doesn't have to be elaborate, but it does have to identify with a target group whose needs are not currently being addressed. The larger the group, the more potential there is for a high return.

There is no reason your operation should be confined to your own campus. Not only are other colleges and universities prime areas, but so are high schools, civic groups, and local businesses.

Brett Johnson, a Harvard graduate, started a million-dollar business in his junior year of college called Crowd Caps that markets painter's caps with logos to large corporations and groups. This is the same idea as T-shirts merely using a different medium. The point is that the potential of this type of business is limited only by the amount of initiative of the owner.

Price.   The pricing of the product is usually determined by local competition. Since you are probably targeting an isolated niche whose needs are not being met, you should consider competition to be T-shirts with the standard college logo sold at the campus book store. If you get a sense that the market will bear a premium price over and above the book store price, act accordingly, but be careful not to price yourself out of the market. If you do so, you may find it difficult to reenter, even at a lower price. Often acquiring the reputation of being a ripoff is too great an obstacle to overcome and still make a profit. What happens is that you must discount so heavily in order to overcome the price-gouge image that worthwhile profits are all but impossible to make.

One thing to note, however, is that whereas many businesses have fixed and variable costs, the T-shirt business has primarily variable costs, depending on how many T-shirts you buy. This is because overhead costs can be minimal and should not be incurred unless large justifiable profits are at stake. Businesses that are primarily variable-cost-oriented are less risky since variable costs are incurred only when sales are made.

Place. The distribution of your T-shirts depends heavily on the unique situation of your school. Some schools may let you set up a booth in the dining hall; others may let you leave an order box in the mailroom. Many colleges or graduate schools have alumni offices whose purpose is to perpetuate school spirit; they might put an advertising blurb in the alumni magazine, thereby tapping the alumni market for your business. Stu Patterson feels that using available school resources is a key path to profitability. Taking advantage of the alumni office, copy machines, student mailboxes, and the dining hall all make life considerably easier at little or no cost. These resources save time, too, since it's easier, for example, to go to the school copy center than to drive into town when making order forms.

An additional distribution resource is the college book store. Selling to the college book store makes you a wholesaler, and you must remember that the book store manager is your immediate customer. Consequently, you must anticipate that he or she will buy in volume and therefore you must discount accordingly to allow room for addition of a 50- to 100-percent markup.

Promotion. The beauty of a T-shirt business is that there is little need for a vast promotional effort, which often can be the most time-consuming and costly component of the marketing effort. If you have selected proper channels of distribution and have selected a message for your T-shirts that stimulates desire to purchase, there is little to be gained from an elaborate promotion effort. This saves you not only time but also money. However, this can change if your objectives are grandiose and your strategy emphasizes aggressiveness.

If you choose to expand your business aggressively into more than what is described here, you will have to rely on promotion to get you where you want to go. This involves a multitude of activities such as giving freebies to visible campus personalities on the condition that they wear them at least once a week to stimulate demand. In addition, you will want to hire a campus rep sales force and supply them with advertising leaflets to stuff into mailboxes or other centers of student activity. Experiment with holding sales contests for your campus reps to get their competitive juices flowing. The only constraint on effective promotional activities is your own imagination.

Conclusion

This is a "quick and dirty" type of student business, ideally suited for graduate students or those who have little time to invest. Although it may contain a significant amount of upward potential, I have chosen to emphasize its ease of implementation and management. If you choose to run with this one, there are not many things you do differently except manage a large number of campus reps on other campuses. Whatever your objective, this can be an enjoyable way to gain basic, practical business experience. At the very least, the experience should help you land an attractive job after school—provided you aren't so enamored with the entrepreneurial process that you strike out on your own.

College Pro

If you like the idea of entrepreneurial freedom and its earnings potential but don't want to expose yourself to excess risk, you may be interested in knowing about College Pro™. College Pro is a corporation that puts college students in business for themselves with house-painting services using methodology that College Pro has refined and perfected for more than a decade. The benefit for you is that College Pro will train you at its expense as well as negotiate favorable terms and conditions with suppliers using its national buying power as leverage. Furthermore, it will supply you with equipment, provide a computerized payroll service for your employees, and generally be available for advice should you require it. The benefit for College Pro is that it makes money from a franchise fee that it charges you, which is based upon a percentage of your business labor hours. The labor hours in turn are directly proportional to the amount of revenue you take in. The motto that College Pro espouses is "Be in business for yourself, but not by yourself."

College Pro is based in Toronto, Canada. Started by 28-year-old Greig Clark, who is currently chairman of the board, College Pro is a corporation with annual revenues of over $12 million that is owned and run by an enterprising group of individuals, all of whom are in their early 20s. In 1982 College Pro painting services painted over 15,000 houses as well as many commercial and institutional structures.

The strategy that College Pro utilizes is that a service like summer house painting is very adaptable to the McDonald's approach of standardization. The more it improves the efficiency of its methodology, the more it can reduce its prices to gain additional customers, yielding still higher profits for all involved. The added advantage is that by publicizing its name it is beginning to cultivate brand loyalty in a line of business that has traditionally been dominated by small, independent, and often unheard-of painting/contractor services.

The advantages to starting your painting service through College Pro are many. First, using films and classroom instruction, the company will train you over the winter and spring months in basic business fundamentals related to its painting services, as well as pigments and other technical aspects of painting that are relevant to the business. Also, you won't have a large up-front investment because College Pro pays for your training, arranges credit terms with suppliers, and generally minimizes your up-front cash needs. One thing you do need is a car. A van is preferable, but cars as small as a VW Rabbit have been known to do the job. Another advantage is that College Pro itself hires regional and national managers from among its student-run painting businesses to help you run your service. One manager I spoke to was 21 years old and had presided over a region that had grossed $700,000 that summer. Thus, the potential exists to move within the structure and broaden your experience. In addition, the method has been proven over the years so that you benefit from more than 10 years of experience even though you yourself may have none. Last, but certainly not least, the potential to make an extremely large income is very high. The average College Pro business makes net profits of between $4,000 and $7,000 in a summer. Some of the more aggressive owners go after industrial customers, and one student in 1982 even landed the contract to paint all of Drew University; the contract was valued at several hundred thousand dollars. So, as you can see, your earnings potential is limited only by your own initiative.

You may be thinking that much of this sounds too good to be true and there has to be another side of the coin. I'll tell you what I see as potential drawbacks. First, while in the practical end of things you are indeed running your own business, College Pro does ask you to conform to certain guidelines, so in the purest theoretical sense of entrepreneurship you don't have 100-percent freedom. However, what they require of you is ultimately in your own best interest—wearing College Pro T-shirts to promote the name, for example. You also have to use its payroll service, for that is how the company records the percent-of-labor franchise fee that you must pay. However, when it comes to the decisions that matter, you are in control. You do your own hiring and firing, market penetration strategy, bookkeeping, and general management. If you want help from College Pro, the company will be glad to assist you, but it generally stays out of your hair unless you need it.

A second possible disadvantage is that in all honesty you will have to work hard and budget your time effectively. It can easily require 15 hours per day to get your business up and running with three or four painting crews in operation working on different jobs. But to be candid, most of the successful ventures that I started required that kind of time also, so I don't think hard work is unique to College Pro.

You should be aware that College Pro is a seasonal business. If you are looking for a business to run during the school year or even year round, painting probably isn't your best bet. But if you are highly academically motivated and want to spend most of your free time during school on homework, College Pro offers an opportunity to get involved in student business and still spend the school year concentrating on academics.

There are fantastic management opportunities at College Pro should you be interested in getting involved in the organization after a summer of running your own painting service. The first level is what College Pro calls zone managers. These are managers who are given a geographical area capable of supporting two or three painting services. Then it is up to the zone managers to find others like themselves who may want to start their own painting services. Zone managers receive a royalty based upon the royalty fee that businesses in the area pay to College Pro based upon the volume of work they do. The earnings of zone managers average between $5,000 and $9,000 per season. Not bad for a summer.

The next level of management is a metro manager, who oversees a metropolitan area or large territory such as Seattle, Boston, Toronto, or Vancouver. This entails working with 25 to 30 separate College Pro painting services. Thus, you must schedule all recruiting and winter training and provide consultation during the summer months. The responsibility is greater, but so is the earnings potential: an average of $9,000 to $15,000 per metro manager for the summer and training periods. Other jobs include field consultant to College Pro business owners, marketing manager, and production manager.

These jobs are good for those of you who want to make a comparatively high summer income and gain tremendous work experience. I know of no other organization that will offer a position equivalent to metro manager to students in their late teens or early 20s. There simply aren't many ways through the traditional summer job search that a college student can get that kind of management responsibility. I don't think I need to overemphasize how powerful an experience like this can look on one's résumé.

Following is a list of addresses so that you may write to College Pro and obtain additional information. You may decide that it is exactly what you are looking for, or you may decide that it doesn't fit your needs. However, you will never know unless you look into it. After all, a postage stamp is hardly a large investment. You might mention that you heard of them through this book so that they know you have some background knowledge of student enterprise.

The addresses are:

National Headquarters: College Pro, 2000 Bathurst Street, Toronto, Ontario M5P 3LI, Canada. (416) 787–0684. Write to Greig Clark.

New England office: 5 Bridge Street, Watertown, MA 02172.

New York office: 130 Metro Park, Rochester, NY 14623. (716) 424–6516.

West Coast office: 2475 Manitoba Street, Vancouver, British Columbia V54 3A4, Canada (604) 879–4105.

DJ Service

A DJ service is made to order for those of you who enjoy stereos, music, and parties. Because hiring a band is prohibitively expensive for most college and social parties, many people turn to a disk jockey, otherwise known as a DJ. Because he or she provides the principal form of entertainment at a party—music to dance to—the DJ is the orchestra leader setting the tone and mood. These are crucial to the success of a party, and many people will pay good money to get a reliable, proven DJ who provides a popular selection of music.

A disk jockey service can be quite profitable aside from being a lot of fun. Once your business is up and running there are minimal variable costs, so when you do a party most of the fee goes right into your pocket. The only expense you incur is gas to get you where you have to go and additional record albums to supplement your collection. Thus, if you charge $100 (not an uncommon fee) you can expect to pocket about 85 percent of it. If you break it down by hour, you would find that you probably average anywhere from $12 to $15 per hour. That's not a bad rate for a part-time business.

The other advantage of a DJ business is that it is a lot of fun. A friend of mine, Scott Jordan, of Los Angeles, ran a very successful DJ business while he was going to college on the East Coast. He also met and dated more women than anyone I knew, all as a result of providing a DJ service at parties every weekend. So if you want to have a lot of fun as well as make money, one area to consider is a DJ service or some other form of party business.

Getting Started

The biggest hurdle to getting into the disk jockey business is the initial startup costs. Aside from a car, it should be fairly apparent that you need a credible stereo system. Most important, though, you need a good collection of popular music that is easy to dance to. Records are more important than the stereo—you can always rent an amplifier and speakers but you can't rent 150 good party albums.

Many of you may already have a powerful stereo system, but for those who don't or who aren't sure if what they've got is adequate, here are some technical details. The amplifier should give you at least 100 watts per speaker, which is adequate for most large rooms. A reasonably good-quality amp of this caliber should cost roughly $1,000. Next you need two turntables, because if you have only one there will be painfully long periods of silence as you change albums. With two turntables you always have the next album on deck and are one song ahead. You may try to borrow or rent a turntable from a friend or classmate if you own only one. Along with turntables you may wish to get a mixer so that when changing songs one song blends into another in a continuous flow of music. However, a mixer is an optional item and can always be acquired later on when profits roll in. The last item on the list is speakers. If you get a large enough pair of speakers you will only need two to do the trick. Obviously, you need speakers that can handle 100 watts or more without blowing a woofer or tweeter. On the other hand, large speakers can usually be rented for roughly $60 per weekend for a pair.

That is a quick rundown on the technical requirements of the business. You will also need about 100 feet of extension cord to reach electrical outlets as well as a high-intensity reading lamp that focuses light in a specific direction. The lamp allows you to see what records you are putting on if the sponsors of a party have turned down the lights. The total cost for all of the mentioned equipment is roughly $2,000. However, if you want to minimize your up-front costs, you can rent speakers and do without the mixer, which reduces startup costs to approximately $1,200. Undoubtedly, many of you already have stereo systems that could be incorporated into a DJ system to reduce startup costs further.

Marketing

Product. Carefully think about the nature of your product, especially in this case where you are providing a fairly homogeneous service (that is, your *Clash* album is just like the next guy's). You must think of yourself as providing more than just music. You are providing entertainment and in fact serve as the mood conductor of the party. In time you can even think of yourself as an insurance policy of credibility. If you establish a reputation of playing good music that gets the crowd hopping, people will associate you with a good time. People begin to think that if you are playing at such and such a party, it has to be good.

Whatever you do, don't think of yourself as just a provider of music. If others see you the same way, they will just rent some big speakers, borrow an amplifier, and make a party tape—for about half what it would cost to get you if you charge $100 or more. Some people like to incorporate a little personality into their service by making dedications before every tune. This is a unique feature and is good as long as it doesn't get overdone. Don't get caught up in the spotlight and think that everyone has come to see you. They haven't. They have come to party.

Remember that every host or hostess wants his or her party to be the best. If you persuade sponsors that your product will make their party fly, you've got a customer. People don't want you to be so different that you'll jeopardize their party, but neither do they want people going home afterward thinking, "Same old thing."

Make sure that you select your music with the crowd you're playing to in mind. A young professional crowd enjoys a different type of music from a high school audience. A young professional crowd also pays a lot more for their DJ needs; they have more money to spend, and image and status are very important at that age. If I were running a DJ service, I'd probably go after the young professional crowd and buy my albums accordingly. However, you may have a particular "in" with a certain crowd and find it easier to market to them. But remember, target your market and design your product around *your customers'* needs, not yours.

Price. The price of your DJ service is a factor of the target market you aim for. For instance, the price you get for doing a Junior League dance will undoubtedly be too high for a college fraternity. Directly related to this issue is the availability of a substitute for your services. A college fraternity undoubtedly has some members who own high-powered stereo gear that may not have fancy turntables or mixers, but they also don't cost the frat any money.

Scott Jordan, whom I mentioned earlier, cleverly targeted the international groups on various campuses. They generally were composed of wealthier students who did not have a problem paying his $100-per-night fee. Also, they preferred a repertoire of songs that were international in nature, which few commercial DJs had. Scott had picked his niche and it worked quite well for him.

The point here is that the fee you charge is very much related to the market you cater to. If you target a range of groups, you may very well have to have a multitiered price structure with one price for high school dances, another for college parties, and so on. My research has shown that high school dances pay roughly $30 to $70, college parties $75 to $125, and young professional parties $200 to $300. You will have to do a little market research to see what your surrounding area will pay and what the competition charges.

Promotion. A DJ service pretty much sells itself. The best promotion for your service is to play some pretty good music at parties and let people at the party know who is responsible—*you.* The trick is letting your audience know about your service without giving your customers the impression that your interests lie in promoting yourself rather more than their party. One suggestion is to leave a stack of business cards on the table where you've set up your equipment. A rather clever method that I've heard can be quite successful is to hold a raffle at a party whereby all guests fill out a card with their name and address. At the end of the night you pick a card and announce the winner. You also have a damned good mailing list at the end of the night, to which you can send a promotional mailing. Even if the bulk of the list is partygoers rather than party-givers you have gotten your name out to a circle of people who will be able to recommend your service to their party-giving friends.

Since the product is all-important, the best way to get yourself started is to offer low price or free trials. By this I mean play for free to a select group of organizations to make your name known as well as to be able to give a credible group of references to prospective customers. Once you have established yourself and the quality of your service, you can begin charging your fee. However, don't go overboard on the freebies, and be sure your selected organizations know that your free service isn't going to be free forever. If the parties you play at turn out to be successful, the hosts may be only too glad to pay for your service as an assurance of future successful functions.

Another method of promotion is to have a couple of thousand matchbooks made up with your name, logo, and advertising message to distribute at parties, where people typically smoke more than usual. This usually costs under $100. Look in the Yellow Pages to find a firm that specializes in matchbook promotions. Or you could just examine the next matchbook you see. Manufacturers often put their name and address at the very bottom.

This is by no means a definitive list of promotional activities. Use your imagination to think of new ways of telling your target market about your services and getting them to try you. If they try the service once and like it, they'll be back for more.

Place.   Since this is a low-volume service business (there are only two nights in a weekend) that caters to a select group of customers (hosts of parties), you really don't need a specific place of distribution outside of your room or apartment. However, an answering machine for your telephone or reliable roommates who take messages are vital. The only contact a potential customer may have with you is that phone call that he or she places to get information or to arrange a date for you to play. Thus, if an image of unreliability is communicated, you're off to a very bad start. What's more, you surely do not want to miss out on a party merely because no one answered the phone or you didn't get the message. Thus, you want to be sure you provide a mechanism to get the message to you with minimal margin for error.

Again, you might want to give some creative thought to new ways of distributing your services that buck the conventional ways of DJ services. You never know, you might discover some new alternative that gives you a distinctive niche in the market.

Conclusion

The DJ business can yield a very profitable return if you overcome the relatively high cost of initial startup. Certainly if you own some or all of the necessary equipment, you have a major advantage. The important points to remember are that targeting a market and playing the appropriate music are key steps to success. Keep an eye on the competition for pricing guidelines, and remember that the product sells itself after a while. If you follow these guidelines, you stand a chance of making good money during the school year and summer months.

Refrigerator Rental Business

A refrigerator rental business offers a distinct advantage over most other student ventures, which is the ability to earn up to several thousand dollars in a very short period of time. The beauty of this business is its simplicity. Once you have your operation set up, the entire process should take you three to four days (conveniently timed before the school year begins) and two days at the end of the school year. In return for this low demand on your time you should net between $15 and $20 per rental, which means you can earn $350 if you have a poor response (20 rentals), $1,050 if you have a medium response (60 rentals), and $1,750 and up if you have a good response (100-plus rentals).

Three critical factors make this business work: lining up a supplier of 2-by-2-by-2-foot fridges, an effective sales blitz, and tight controls and record keeping so that you know where your fridges are and how to contact your renters. It may sound idiotic, but you'd be amazed how easy it is to lose track of a refrigerator when you are unloading 60 or 70 of them for delivery in a matter of hours. Every lost unit is $150 right out of profits, which is frustrating and painful.

Getting Started

The first thing you need to do is survey neighboring schools to see whose needs aren't being met. Many universities have discovered this little gold mine and do it themselves through their various student agencies. However, many schools do not, and I found plenty of opportunities while I was in the Boston area, including my own school, Babson. My experience showed that the unserviced niches were typically small- to medium-sized schools, especially all-female schools, though

I'm not sure why. The large schools present such tempting profits that virtually all are being serviced. Thus, you have to take a look at your own school and others to see where the opportunity lies. You should also look up a competitor at a nearby school and find what the going rate for a yearly rental is so that you can competitively price your service. You might even find that someone is vulnerable to a low-cost supplier should you elect to lock horns in competitive battle. Unless there are no other uncovered campuses, I do not recommend head-on cost competition because they can turn around and match your price overnight and eliminate the competitive advantage you briefly held. This quickly becomes a battle of who can undercut the most, which then boils down to who has the financial staying power.

Once you have done market research that reveals an opportunity, you must line up a supplier or buy your own refrigerators. There is no clear-cut way to find a mass supplier of fridges, for many are run by entrepreneurial types out of their homes. We found ours because my partner went to a large neighboring women's college to visit his sister and saw the supplier's advertising leaflet. We called and, in essence, rented wholesale and then rerented the fridges with a profit margin built in. Some suppliers advertise but many don't. Finding a supplier will in all likelihood be the most difficult part of the operation, but persist and ye shall find. Try calling the refrigerator manufacturers to see if anyone has bought 500 to 1,000 refrigerators recently for purposes of renting to colleges. If there is no one in your area and there are several colleges or universities within 30 miles, you could be on to a much bigger opportunity than what I'm envisioning in this chapter—you could be the supplier for the whole area. This probably won't happen often, but if it does you should engage professional advice that is attuned to the particulars of the situation.

The other method of supply that we used was buying our own units in addition to renting. The key is to buy a number of units that you will always be able to rent, thus shifting the risk of fluctuations in demand to the wholesale supplier of rentals. For instance, we owned 12 of our own units. We were currently renting out 45 to 60 units per year (although we hit 103 my senior year). We were always sure that the first 12 orders we got were filled with our own units, which we did not have to pay a rental fee for. Thus, all the money went into our pockets. If demand had dropped to 20 units, it would have been the supplier who would be stuck with unused refrigerators, not us. This approach necessitates an up-front capital expenditure, which may not always be feasible. However, the other advantage, aside from not paying a rental fee to the supplier, is that you can rent yours out during college summer sessions so that the little suckers are earning money for you year-round. In either case, the risks are not great so long as you leave a comfortable margin for error between what you own and the level of demand. If you rent all of your own refrigerators, there is virtually no risk other than loss due to negligence in bookkeeping or theft (which is rare).

You should also get a contract drawn up that you will have your customers sign specifying that (1) you own or are renting the refrigerator, (2) the lessee is fully responsible for the unit and will be charged in full for any and all damages, (3) you will pick the unit up on or by a specified date, (4) the amount the lessee is paying for the rental and the amount of damage deposit you require. This ensures that no one tries to say that the "rented" refrigerator is really theirs and you are trying to pull a quick one. It also ensures that you've got something legally viable so that you can collect damages if someone breaks the unit.

Marketing

The product in and of itself is simple enough. Promotion and distribution are certainly factors, but the key to marketing refrigerator rentals is price. A small refrigerator costs roughly $130 from a discount mass merchandiser. Thus, your competition is frequently the option a prospective customer has to purchase his or her refrigerator rather than rent yours. Obviously a key component of the pricing decision is your lease cost. You must strive to keep your price, including profit margin, under $55 per year, or approximately 40 percent of retail

200

sale price. One interesting way to circumvent a high yearly rental price is to break your fee down into a semester rental price, front-loaded in the fall semester so that the probabilities of rerental are high.

For example, if you have a $55 yearly rental fee, you structure a price schedule that might be $40 for the fall semester and $15 for the spring. Thus, the initial cash outlay by the consumer is not as high as it would be if he or she rented for a full year of $55. Moreover, when it comes time to renew the contract it should not be too hard to persuade him or her that $15 for a semester is a great deal (less than $1.50 per week!).

Promotion is the other key variable. You have about two weeks to get in and get your orders, so it's very important that you carefully plan this activity during the summer months. You have to obtain permission from colleges and universities that you intend to canvass, which can sometimes be time-consuming. Design an advertising leaflet that you can have copied at a copying center for 5 cents per copy. If you plan to hit several campuses, it is highly advisable to hire a student sales rep who attends the given institution and who can distribute leaflets for you. Moreover, local reps know the ins and outs and know the right places for posters, whom to contact for permission, and other information. If you operate through this person, your chances for administration approval are improved since the venture is seen as the student's venture and not an outsider trying to make some money off the student body.

Sophisticated promotion such as newspaper advertising is unnecessary and frequently not cost-justified. The best promotion is a good compensation plan that gets your reps working their little tails off. A good rep is almost priceless. A bad one is an opportunity cost, as it's too late when you discover the error, and you won't get another shot until next year.

Keeping Records

Poor record keeping can eliminate your profits very quickly. The higher your volume, the more vital it is to set up a procedure before you begin deliveries. You should record the serial number of the refrigerator (to make sure someone doesn't pull a switch on you), the name of the customer, address, and phone number. The list and signed contracts upon completion of your deliveries are extremely valuable, since they are all you have to go on for picking up the units at the end of the spring semester. Lose those and you'll be very sorry, so make a copy and keep one in a very secure place. I once misplaced mine for an extremely anxious couple of days.

In summary, this can be a very lucrative business with little demand on your time, which is especially attractive if you're a serious student. The keys are getting a good supplier, competitive prices, and reps who will hustle on their respective campuses. The timetable looks like this:

Spring semester of preceding year:
- Line up supplier.
- Survey surrounding colleges and universities.
- Select targeted campuses.
- Pick sales reps.

During summer:
- Stay in touch with reps and determine when everyone will be back on campus and how early reps can get into housing units to begin putting up publicity before everyone arrives.
- Design advertising leaflet.
- Draw up contract.

Beginning of fall semester:
- Begin poster and leaflet advertising blitz.
- Reps begin taking orders.
- Tally final orders, call in order to supplier.
- Make deliveries.

End of spring semester:
- Make phone calls to customers informing

them of date and time of pickup (this can also be assigned to the sales rep).

- Pick up units and return deposits.
- Clean units.
- Schedule pickup from supplier.

CHAPTER 10

Getting a Job or
Getting into Grad School

Many of the benefits of running your own business are realized not while you're in college but rather when you leave the academic community. There are generally three paths you will follow: getting a job, going on to graduate school, or continuing to run your student business on a full-time basis. Much of making college pay lies in what a college experience does for your future.

As I have stressed throughout this book, there are many distinct advantages to running your own business in school, and it is important that you use those advantages as leverage once you graduate. You will find that the attributes you acquire and develop can be very powerful tools if you should look for a job in business or entertain thoughts of applying to graduate business schools. Part of the rationale for the perceived weight of these characteristics is that there is a very small percentage of students who go the entrepreneurial route and, by virtue of their minority status, are able to present a unique story about themselves. Moreover, a student business gives you that most elusive of desired characteristics—management experience.

There are four critical attributes that you should stress in interviews and in graduate business school applications. The first is general management skills. Unlike most of your classmates, you will have hands-on general management experience. Making decisions, dealing with people, and having an overall understanding of the big picture are all attributes that employers look upon with favor. Dealing with people is particularly important to many companies, as the bulk of the internal problems of a firm are people problems. Thus, someone who has a proven track record of dealing with people, either employees or the general public, significantly lowers the level of risk associated with a new hire and thus gives you an edge.

Also important is understanding the big picture. Any candidate for a job who explains he or she ran a business in college and thus understands some of what the boss has to go through in running an organization will impress the hell out of an interviewer. Explaining that you understand that you are a part of the picture but not the center of the universe demonstrates your maturity in grasping the organization's overall goals.

The second key attribute is maturity. Lack of maturity is considered to be one of the biggest reasons a high percentage of newly hired college graduates leave their first job within a year. Looking at the issue through the eyes of a corporate personnel recruiter, the worst thing for them is to have a new hire quit before he or she is up to speed. Thus, attributes that reduce this risk are given considerable attention. Running your own business takes a level of maturity and street smarts that no level of success in the classroom can match. It takes commitment and the ability to weather the bad times as well as the good. This comparative advantage is one that you should point out during an interview, because it puts you on the same ground as the highest academic performer in the class. In fact, it even puts you a little higher because street smarts are an intangible strength that cannot be obtained in the classroom. Knowing how to cut a business deal so that you leave as little as possible on the bargaining table is a process you probably went through when negotiating with your suppliers and one that few of your classmates will be able to match.

The third attribute that you should stress when you're being interviewed is initiative. *Initiative* is a good word to recruiters. It means you take the ball and run with it without looking for advice every 10 minutes. It means that you look for work rather than sitting in your office waiting for it to find you. Initiative is a particularly powerful attribute if you are considering any kind of job that has a fair degree of autonomy such as selling or consulting. The demonstrated ability to manage your own time is highly regarded by those who hire. After all, if you were hiring a manager for your student business, wouldn't you favor the candidate who had a proven record of initiative?

The last important attribute when interviewing for a job is confidence. If you have any success at all as a student business owner, you should feel very proud of yourself. Even if a venture fails, you can feel pride, because you will have learned valuable lessons. (In some cases I learned more from my failures than from my successes.) Better to have tried and lost than never to have tried at all. You should feel good about your student venture and recognize it as a true accomplishment. All employers like winners; who doesn't? Anyone who has an air of self-confidence will naturally project a favorable image. Projecting a positive image is the name of the game when it comes to getting a job or applying to graduate business school.

Getting a Job

Having seen stacks of résumés from prospective applicants when I worked at Boeing, I can't stress enough the degree to which the vast majority of them look alike. The ability to have a résumé that sticks out is vital. One key way to stand out is to stress your student business experience and the previously mentioned attributes. If your sales volume is over $5,000, you might want to include it in the description of your business, which should be described in your résumé under work experience. Give yourself a title that is descriptive but not overly pompous. Titles such as chairman of the board and chief executive officer imply that you're living in a world of titles that befit a corporation such as General Motors. A more realistic strategy is to understate your title (founder, president, and director are good for this) and then hammer home your job duties. Emphasize your responsibility for setting objectives, determining strategy, and managing employees. Companies are not so concerned with titles as they are with work experience and transferable skills. Another area to stress is your rate of growth, which in percentage terms is bound to be high, since in the early days of a new business a low increase in dollar volume can still yield a significantly high percentage. Associated with these data can be information pertaining to the markets you targeted and new markets subsequently pursued. The larger your business, the more you have to work with in presenting a positive impression of yourself. In short, tell the story of your business; don't just tack it on the end with a two-sentence description.

One reservation about a student business owner that some recruiters might harbor concerns the entrepreneurial traits of independence and nonconformity. However, these are easily defused. The first point you can make to someone who shows signs of apprehension about your entrepreneurial background is that student businesses operate under the relative security of the academic environment. After all, if your business folds you merely continue to pursue your studies, which was your primary purpose anyway. This contrasts vividly with real life, where a business foldup is usually accompanied by bankruptcy and unemployment. Moreover, a true entrepreneurial venture entails risk, whereas in the world of student business the risk is sharply reduced. Another point for you to make is the motivation you had for starting your business in the first place.

One reason I frequently gave was that I couldn't find any kind of work experience that gave me the breadth of responsibility that a student venture did. Surely working in the cafeteria or gymnasium did not provide the intellectual challenges, let alone the monetary rewards, that my student businesses offered.

Another justification for running your own business in school is the flexibility in working hours, which traditional part-time college jobs generally don't have. Being able to choose your own hours is important, particularly during midterms, finals, and term papers. Moreover, when your academic schedule changes every semester it is awfully difficult to get the same level of responsibility that you get with running your own business. Often I would hear classmates complaining that just as they were getting enough seniority to take over managing their employer's afternoon shift, the semester would end and they would have a totally new class schedule, which necessitated their moving to a new area of the company.

A third and quite effective reason for starting your own business that any recruiter should understand is that you needed to make money because of the increased cost of getting a college education. Anyone who has read a paper or a newsmagazine within the last three years should be aware of this phenomenon. There are few opportunities in which you can make as much money as you can with a well-run student business in a comparatively small amount of time. Indeed, the decision to run your own student business in college can be made to look like the most obvious, logical decision a student should make.

When interviewing, let the interviewer be the first to bring up the subject of your entrepreneurial experience, which he or she should do if you position it correctly in your résumé. If after a while no mention is made, it is up to you to throw it in casually to see how much interest is generated. You are unlikely ever to find an interviewer who has no interest and does not want to hear more about your ventures. Whenever you talk about a specific venture, conclude with one or two key lessons in management that you learned. This demonstrates experience and maturity. Use the soft sell, though, and don't flood the conversation with detail. The interviewer may also be looking to see how well-rounded you are, and your ability to converse on different topics is a clue.

When you apply for a job, try to think of the interview as one big glorified sales call. You are now selling the ultimate product—you. Refer back to the chapter on selling for some basic tools and perspectives that are helpful in an interview. You are selling the interviewer on the idea that the best labor he or she can possibly buy is you. Half the fear and nervousness that people associate with interviews is caused by their getting too emotionally involved in the process. Every interview is a sales call and, remember, selling is a game of numbers. The more sales calls you make, the higher the probability that one of those sales calls will produce a sale. One of the advantages of owning your own student business is the experience in selling, which should give you an edge in the interview process.

Graduate School

The other area in which student business experience offers you a definite competitive edge in is applying to graduate business school. Not everyone does graduate work in business, if they go to graduate school at all, but the fact remains that an M.B.A. or equivalent is one of the most popular degrees and the competition for admission is fierce. Applying to graduate business schools is a long and often traumatic experience, but an advantage of the written application is that, unlike an interview that depends on spontaneity, a written application allows you to rewrite your answers and essays as many times as you like until you've got them just right. This is an advantage that plays to your student enterprise experience. It allows you to line up your ducks just right so that you can present your story with maximum impact. Thus, you should carefully think of the important facts and impressive figures you want to stress and organize a concise, well-worded, powerful essay. It is very important, though, that you tell the story and don't just write a two-sentence summary. Give facts, figures, growth rates, and all other pertinent information.

Graduate business schools like entrepreneurial experience. One reason is that the majority of schools look upon their mission as educating tomorrow's leaders, not followers. Running your own business is about the best way of stating at an early age that you intend to be a business leader, not a cog in the wheel.

A second reason entrepreneurial experience is a positive influence on an admissions committee is that it displays independence and willingness to take a risk. Thus, in applying to B school you have to stress the risks you took, although they may take a form other than money, such as time or specific lost opportunities.

An additional reason student business experience is helpful is that most schools ask you why you want to go to business school in the first place. Although it seems like a pretty obvious question with an obvious answer, you have an excellent opportunity to give not just an obvious response but an excellent one. Running a student business allows you to see what necessary formal learning tools you need to augment your experience. Your application implies that you understand the value of the formal, integrated, broad business curriculum graduate business schools offer. Stress that running your own business showed you how ill-equipped you were with the technical tools that are available in grad school. As an example, I wrote that I had been woefully deficient in understanding leverage financing, which would have helped me when I was expanding my publishing business into a full-time operation. Gaining access to such knowledge, I stated, was a primary reason for applying to business school.

It is vital that you have a credible (and motivating) reason for wanting to attend business school. Many people apply merely because they haven't got anything better to do, and it shows on their applications. Applying to business school just because you don't like your current job is not a good enough reason; a good reason is a desire to absorb knowledge that you now know is important.

Moreover, should you not be a scholar with a 4.0 grade point average, a credible student business is a powerful rationale for not achieving a strong academic record. After all, the temptations of money and responsibility have been known to capture the soul of many a virtuous individual, so you certainly would not be the first. Graduate school provides an opportunity to drink in knowledge forfeited during undergraduate years when you were running your own business.

One note of caution: don't misperceive a student business as a guarantee of a job or admission to a graduate business school. What it does guarantee, if presented correctly, is that you will be better positioned than your peers. You will stand out. However, your background is only one of several factors in a decision. A student business merely improves your chances. That's all. The better your chances, the fewer doors you'll have to knock on when it comes time to get a job or apply to business school. Getting a good job or getting into grad school is part of making college pay.

GLOSSARY

Accounting. A system for recording financial transactions of a company or entity.

Accounting period. A period of time over which financial records are summarized. Normal accounting periods for student ventures are months, semesters, or a school year.

Accounts payable. The amounts owed to firms that have extended you credit. This is considered a current liability on the balance sheet.

Accounts receivable. The amounts owed to you by students or firms with whom you do business. This is classified as a current asset on the balance sheet.

Advertising. Efforts made to stimulate sales through mass media, usually the college newspaper. However, colored mimeographed sheets are often cheaper and can be as effective. Advertising can take many forms; the objective is to develop the mix that gets the best results. (*See* **Promotion.**)

Annuity. An agreement whereby a series of fixed monetary payments are made at specified intervals over a determined period of time.

Asset. Anything of value owned by the company. Assets generally fall into three categories: current assets, which can be expected to be converted into cash within one year; fixed assets, which cannot be easily converted into cash; and intangible assets, which include such things as patents, licenses, goodwill, and so on.

Balance sheet. A statement of financial position that displays a company's assets, liabilities, and owner's equity. A balance sheet always balances according to this equation: Assets = Liabilities + Owner's equity.

Bankruptcy. The ultimate mistake. Bankruptcy occurs when you are no longer able to pay your creditors.

Book value. As applied to an asset, book value is the value you assign a given asset on your balance sheet. As applied to a company, book value is assets minus liabilities.

Bottom line. The net after-tax income your company reports on the "bottom line" of the income statement.

Break-even point. The amount of units that must be sold before the company shows a profit. All fixed and variable expenses must have been covered.

Budget. The planning of expenses in order to control costs.

Capital. The investment in a company so that it can conduct its business. Capital can be raised through owner investment, issuing stock, issuing bonds, or other forms of debt.

Capital-intensive. Describes an industry or firm that requires a great deal of investment to stay in business. The car industry is considered capital-intensive because it takes a great deal of capital to enter into as well as maintain. (*See* **Labor-intensive.**)

Cash. Actual money in the bank available to spend.

Cash flow. The actual amount of cash generated by business operations over a specific period of time. Cash flow differs from profits because some expenses may be incurred but not paid in a given time period.

Commission. A fee paid to a salesperson, agent, or broker, usually as a percentage of sales or profits.

Compound interest. Interest paid on principal and left on deposit so that it will itself earn interest in succeeding periods.

Consignment. An arrangement with the seller of goods (retail stores) whereby the seller does not take title to or pay for the goods until they are sold and has the option of returning them to the supplier.

Contribution (margin). The difference between the sales price of a product or service and its associated variable cost. The contribution covers fixed expenses and profit.

Corporation. A legal organization chartered by the state. The primary advantage to a corporation is that liability is limited only to the amount you invest. The disadvantage is that profits are taxed twice, once as corporate profits and again when you pay personal income tax on the dividends paid to you.

Cost of goods sold (COGS). The actual cost of the product you are selling, and often the major component of variable costs. For businesses with fluctuating inventory costs COGS is computed as follows: COGS = Beginning inventory + Purchases − Ending inventory. In service businesses the cost of goods sold is usually your labor cost.

Credit. The ability to procure goods and services without paying for them until a specified time. This considerably helps cash flow. In accounting a credit is an entry signifying a decrease in an asset account or an increase in a liability or owner's equity account. For further explanation refer to Chapter 8.

Current assets. Asset accounts on the balance sheet that could be converted into cash in one year or less. However, for student businesses the time span, although not official, is usually considered to be one semester.

Current liabilities. Liability accounts on the balance sheet that are due in one year or less, although in student businesses this is usually shortened to one semester.

Debit. An accounting entry signifying an increase in assets or a reduction in liabilities or capital. The opposite of a debit is a credit, and every debit has a balancing credit. (*See* **Credit.**)

Debt. An obligation to pay back an amount owed. (*See* **Liability.**)

Depreciation. An expense that is supposed to reflect the loss of value in a fixed asset such as machinery or a car. It is a non-cash charge and as such is solely a bookkeeping entry. There are several methods of depreciation, the simplest of which is straight-line depreciation (dividing the asset value by the life expectancy of the asset). For instance, a $100 machine with a five-year life would be depreciated at $20 per year.

Distribution. The method by which a company gets its product or service to the ultimate consumer. Also known as channels of distribution. (*See* **Place.**)

Double-entry bookkeeping. A system of accounting reputed to be devised by an Italian monk in medieval times. This system requires that each accounting transaction be entered as a debit and as a credit. Thus the sum of all debits should equal the sum of all credits.

Downside risk. The amount of loss that an investor could experience should all go wrong. Any venture that has a high downside risk should have a large upside potential. (*See* **Upside potential.**)

Eighty/twenty rule. A general theory that 20 percent of your customers will generate 80 percent of your revenues and profits. Efforts should be concentrated on the 20 percent that generates 80 percent of your profits.

Economies of scale. Lowering of costs as an operation becomes bigger. The more product you buy or sell the cheaper each unit cost is, because fixed costs get spread over a larger number of units. Thus, if you buy in volume the seller should pass on some of the realized savings.

Entrepreneur. One who undertakes responsibility and risk to start a venture.

Equity. The owner's stake in the business. Equity is determined by subtracting liabilities from assets.

External financing. Meeting the financial needs of the firm through external sources such as bank loans, borrowing money from friends and family, or issuing stock. (*See* **Internal financing.**)

Financial statement. A report on the financial status of a business. Examples of financial statements are the balance sheet and the income statement.

Fixed assets. Assets used in the conduct of business. Fixed assets typically cannot be readily converted into cash and include such things as machinery, buildings, and land.

Fixed cost. A cost that does not vary with the volume of sales. Fixed costs are incurred whether you sell one unit or 100 units. Used in calculating the break-even point, examples of fixed costs are salaries, interest on debt, rent, and depreciation. (*See* **Variable cost.**)

Goodwill. An intangible asset that is used when a company is acquired for more than its net book value. For instance, if you were to sell your student business for $1,000 but the net book value of the firm was $800, the $200 difference would be classified as goodwill.

Gross margin. Net sales less cost of goods sold equals gross margin. Gross margin is what is left to cover your indirect costs of doing business. Gross margin for most student firms is the same as contribution margin.

Income tax. A tax imposed by government, based on a percentage of earnings for firms or on gross income for individuals.

Inflation. The continued rise in the general price level of the economy. Inflation is measured by increases in the consumer price index, a government statistic that monitors price fluctuations in the economy.

Interest. A rental fee paid for the temporary use of someone else's money. Interest is normally expressed as a percentage of the principal to be paid for use of the money for one year.

Internal financing. The funding of the business's financial requirements through funds generated by operations such as retained profits. (*See* **External financing.**)

Inventory. Goods held for sale or production by the firm. Inventory is classified as a current asset.

Invoice. A billing statement giving a detailed list of goods or services provided.

Journal. Accounting support statements that are posted in chronological order and eventually entered into the general ledger. Examples of journals are the cash journal, accounts payable journal, and accounts receivable journal. (*See* **Ledger.**)

Labor-intensive. A term describing the principal costs of a firm, product, or industry as being largely composed of labor. (*See* **Capital-intensive.**)

Law of supply and demand. A general prevailing theory that states that all markets are controlled by the forces of demand by consumers and by supply forces of firms competing in the market. The balance between supply and demand is referred to as the equilibrium.

Ledger. A record of the firm's financial transactions which is maintained by account. Journal entries are transferred to the ledger. (*See* **Journal.**)

Liabilities. Any debt or obligation owed by a company or person to others. Liabilities are classified into two segments: current liabilities, which are due in the short term, and long-term liabilities, which are due in the far term. Examples of long-term liabilities would be mortgages, bonds, and long-term loans.

Liquidity. The extent to which a firm has cash or current assets easily converted to cash. Investors and creditors usually pay a lot of attention to a company's liquidity and use a liquidity ratio as a tool to measure by. A liquidity ratio is current assets divided by current liabilities. Any liquidity ratio of less than 1.0 means the company cannot pay off all current liabilities with current assets.

Loss leader. A particular product in the product line that is deliberately sold at or below cost in order to induce customers to try the company's product or in the hopes that the customer will also buy additional products that yield profits.

Market. The collective group of individuals or firms that constitute the target purchasers for a given product or service. For example, the college advertiser market is considered to be all organizations and businesses wishing to communicate a message to college students.

Marketing. The collective effort in bringing a product from manufacturer to consumers. These efforts include distribution, promotion, advertising, packaging, and market research.

Marketing mix. The strategic mix of marketing elements that one uses in a overall marketing plan designed to meet set marketing objectives.

Market penetration. A marketing strategy, the objective of which is to generate high-volume sales even at the expense of lowering prices. The underlying objective in this strategy is to gain high market share. (*See* **Market skimming.**)

Market segment. A group or segment within a given market who have certain characteristics such as age, income, geographic location, or consumer attitudes.

Market share. The relationship between a company's total sales and the industry's total sales expressed as a percentage. Market share can be expressed both in terms of dollars or total units sold.

Market skimming. A marketing strategy frequently used with new products whereby only the most profitable market segment is targeted, resulting in high unit prices. In succeeding time periods the company may lower the product's price to draw in new market segments and thus drive up volume and market share.

Net worth. The difference between total assets and total liabilities. This is reflected in the owner's equity section of the balance sheet (Assets − Liabilities = Owner's equity or net worth).

Objective.   A goal or target. A business plan flows from a firm's objectives.

Opportunity cost.   The options forsaken by following a particular course of action. For instance, the decision to focus on a particular market segment may utilize so much of your marketing resources that it may preclude you from entering alternative markets.

Overhead.   A cost that does not vary with sales volume. Overhead includes such things as rent, salaries, insurance, and phone costs. In the student business sector, overhead and fixed costs are often the same. It is very important to keep overhead costs down.

Partnership.   A business structure whereby two or more individuals pool their resources and share the profits of a business venture. The advantage to a partnership is that profits are taxed only once as personal income. The primary disadvantage is that partners are liable for all debts of the firm. Most student businesses are sole proprietorships or two-person partnerships.

Payback period.   A method of evaluating an investment by determining the number of time periods that it will take before the money put into an investment is fully recovered.

Place.   Where customers will buy the product.

Price.   What the product costs. Considerations include competition's price, what the market will bear, quantity discount incentives, as well as others.

Price elasticity.   An economic concept that relates the effect of price to consumer demand. If a change in price results in a large change in demand, a product is said to be elastic; if a change in price has little effect on consumer demand, the product is said to be inelastic.

Prime rate.   The interest rate that banks charge their most creditworthy customers. Prime is considered to be a barometer of interest rates in general.

Principal. The face value or original amount of a loan. Principal can be paid off in one lump payment at the end of a loan or in regular installment payments.

Product. What the company sells, often thought of as a manufactured good, but it can be a service as well.

Profit. The difference between revenues and costs. While often thought of as the main gauge of success of a company, many firms elect to pay high salaries and expenses to their owners, thereby reducing profits. The owners in either case take home the same amount of money.

Pro forma statement. A financial statement that forecasts future financial results. Pro forma statements usually are based upon historical results and are used to help management determine future personnel and cash needs.

Promotion. Efforts to stimulate sales through advertising, posters, direct selling, discounts, and two-for-one specials, for instance.

Proprietorship. A business that has a single owner.

Pull strategy. A marketing strategy designed to influence the ultimate consumer so that the consumer goes to the store and *pulls* your product through the distribution channels. Pull strategies are generally associated with large advertising efforts. For example, if you advertise a discount on your product, consumers will go to the retailer to get it, thus pulling it through the retail distribution channel.

Push strategy. A marketing strategy designed to influence the participants of the distribution channel in order to *push* the product at the consumer. Push strategies are usually associated with large price discounts to merchandisers and retailers that give them high margins, which provides incentive to "push" the product.

Retailer. One who buys products in quantity at lower prices and resells them one at a time for a higher price.

Retained earnings. The cumulative amount of undistributed profits that remain in the company. Retained earnings are seldom in the form of cash; rather, they are used to finance credit to customers and marketing programs, for instance.

Return on equity. A tool used to measure a company's performance that expresses net profits as a percentage of gross owner investment.

Return on investment (ROI). A tool used to measure a company's performance that expresses net profits as a percentage of total investment.

Revenue. The amount of money received or owed to a company for goods or services provided.

Risk. The degree of uncertainty or possibility of a loss. All projects and ventures entail some degree of risk. Generally speaking, low risks yield low returns and high risks require high returns.

Risk-free investment. A barometer used to measure actual risk. Risk-free investments are such things as United States government securities and federally insured bank savings rates. The higher risk-free investment rates are, the higher a return investors will demand for investments that do carry risk, such as investing in International Harvester.

Risk premium. The differential between the risk-free investment rate and the actual rate a lender requires for an investment.

Short-term debt. Debt that must be paid back within one year. With student businesses, it is generally considered to be one semester.

Solvency. The amount by which a firm's current assets exceed its current liabilities. This reflects a company's ability to pay its bills.

Standard deviation. The degree of variation away from the mean. When statistical averaging is done it is often helpful to know how much variance away from the average exists within the data set.

Startup cost. The expense incurred in starting a venture. This includes all costs incurred up to the initial realization of profits.

Stock. The units into which ownership of most firms is usually divided. Ownership of a firm is measured by the amount of stock held as a percentage of total issued stock.

Strategy. The plans used to achieve a set of objectives.

Strategic planning. The process of planning future strategies. In the case of student businesses, planning is usually not necessary for more than two or three semesters in the future.

Sunk cost. Costs that have been spent and are therefore unrecoverable. The concept is that previously spent costs are not relevant to decisions regarding the present or future. Thus the saying to remember is "Sunk costs are sunk."

Synergy. The effect that a group can have by producing more as a group than as a sum of the individuals.

Tactic. The implementation of strategy.

Time value of money. The concept that money is more valuable in the present than in the future due to the eroding effects of inflation as well as lost opportunity.

Upside potential. The most an investment could realize if the best possible outcome were realized. (*See* **Downside risk.**)

Variable costs. Those costs that vary directly in proportion to volume of production or services provided. Variable costs are such things as raw materials, some labor, and shipping.

Venture capital. Investment monies specifically targeted for startup or early stage ventures.

Vertical integration. The expansion by a firm into industries that produce or market the firm's product at different levels.

Wholesaler. The middleman between the manufacturer and the retailer. By going to a wholesaler you cut out the retailer and pocket the difference.

Working capital. Current assets minus current liabilities. Because student businesses are so cash-oriented you may prefer to simply think of it as unspent cash in the bank account.

INDEX